KU-799-893

Andalucía

from end

Gardens

Parks

Museums

History

Eating out

Streets and squares

Monuments

Shopping

to end

Written by: **Fernando Olmedo**

EDICIONES
Aldeasa

Andalucía
from end to end

CASTILLA - LA MANCHA

MURCIA

PROVINCIA DE JAÉN

PROVINCIA DE GRANADA

PROVINCIA DE ALMERÍA

ALMERÍA

SIERRA NEVADA

MAR MEDITERRÁNEO

Costa Tropical

Golfo de Almería

A brief history

The South of Europe

Andalucía is the southernmost region of continental Europe. It extends from the south of the Iberian Peninsula between the Mediterranean and the Atlantic, separated from Africa by the fourteen kilometres of the Straits of Gibraltar. The region covers 87,595 square kilometres, equal in size to countries such as Portugal or Austria and has a population of around seven and a half million inhabitants. Andalucía is one of Spain's seventeen Autonomous Communities, and is divided internally into eight provinces with their respective capitals: Almería, Cádiz, Córdoba, Granada, Huelva, Jaén, Malaga and Seville, the latter the seat of the regional parliament and government.

A land of marked contrasts, Andalucía features an exceptionally wide variety of landscapes, from long beaches and rocky bays to agricultural land, desert, woods and Alpine mountains. The River Guadalquivir forms a great plane of cultivated land in the centre of the region between the gentle mountain range of the Sierra Morena to the north and the steep profile of the Sierra Bética to the south. Rising up in the middle of these mountains is the Sierra Nevada, with the Mulhacén, the highest mountain in Spain at 3,482 metres. In general, Andalucía's climate is Mediterranean, with gentle winters, hot summers, moderate rain and a high sunshine total, almost 3,000 hours per year.

Origins and Antiquity

Archaeologists have proved that human beings were present in Andalucía almost 1 million years ago, when this

The ruins of Baelo Claudia, Tarifa (Cádiz) ▶

region possibly acted as a bridge for the first humans to pass from Africa into Europe. This role of meeting and passing-through point has formed its character ever since. From the Neolithic period onwards it was at the forefront of progress in agriculture, livestock keeping and mining, all of these attracting Greek and Phoenician settlers. This civilising influence gave rise to the Kingdom of Tartesos, famous for its metals, a remote territory in which the Columns of Hercules marked out the borders of the known world. This was followed by the development of Iberian culture in the interior of the region, as well as the presence of the Carthaginian civilisation and the period of Roman rule, which left a permanent influence. Under the Romans, this region became the province of Bética and was the grainstore of the Empire, the location for flourishing cities such as Corduba, the noble capital of the province, or the aristocratic Itálica, birthplace of the Emperors Trajan and Hadrian.

Between East and West

After the brief period of Visigothic rule, the Muslim presence would mark out Andalucía's destiny for almost 800 years to come. Until the 10th century Cordoba, the capital of Al-Andalus (the Muslim region of the Spanish Peninsula) and court of the Ommeyad Caliphs, stood out as the great city in the West. Seville, Almería, Malaga, Jaén and others cities acquired walls, fortresses, mosques, schools, baths, palaces, markets and entire quarters where people of different races and religions lived together. Andalucía enjoyed one of its most splendid periods, as a great cultural beacon between the East and Europe. The advance of the Christian reconquest confined the Muslims to the present limits of the region, and the rapid reconquest of Cordoba, Seville and the Guadalquivir Valley by Ferdinand III in the mid-13th century pushed the Moors towards the eastern realms of the Kingdom of Granada, the last bastion of Islam in the Peninsula, and one which would survive for another 250 years. At this period the frontier wars encouraged the construction of dozens of hill forts and fortified towns, while Hispano-Arabic culture cast its last bright gleams from the Palaces of the Alhambra in Granada.

Aristocrats and Merchants

1492 is a key date in the history of Andalucía. The year began with the conquest of Granada by the Catholic Kings. In the summer, Christopher Columbus set sail from the Andalucían port of Palos in Huelva on route for America. This

Arco de Villalar and Puerta de Jaén, Baeza (Jaén) ▶

was also the year when the Jews were expelled, to be followed in the 17th century by the Moors, depriving the region of two of its most active communities.

In this new context, Andalucía acquired a leading role. The monopoly of trade with South America, which included huge quantities of gold, silver and spices, was established in Seville in 1503, and the city acquired the status of world trading centre. Encouraged by these circumstances, prosperity spread along the cost and inland where the aristocracy had acquired huge estates. In the cities, the new Renaissance and Baroque styles were used to improve the old Medieval layout, and impressive town centres were built in Úbeda and Baeza, as well as cathedral, monasteries and convents, civil constructions and palaces. This was the context for the work of the great artistic geniuses of the region such as Góngora, Velázquez and Murillo.

From the Romantics to the 20th century

In the 18th century Seville lost its status as capital of the overseas colonies in favour of Cadiz, which consequently enjoyed a golden period. The 19th century dawned with a series of key events: the Battle of Trafalgar (Cadiz) in 1805, the defeat of Napoleon's army at Bailén (Jaén) in 1808, the Proclamation of the first Spanish Constitution in Cadiz in 1812, and General Riego's Liberal uprising in Cabezas (Cadiz) in 1820. Remote from these imperial glories, agriculture continued to be the prevailing activity in Andalucía. The region soon began to attract Romantic travellers, charmed by the landscape and its inhabitants. A land of bullfighters and singers, warm and passionate, exotic and friendly, Andalucía was the archetype of Romantic Spain, personified in such famous characters as Carmen, Don Juan and Figaro.

Progressing slowly and painfully towards the modern age, the first decades of the 20th century saw a prosperous and optimistic period, particularly with regard to culture. Picasso, Juan Ramón Jiménez, De Falla, Lorca, Alberti, Cernuda, Aleixandre and others are all great names of Spanish culture who were born in this region. The tragedy of the Civil War cut short hopes and expectations. The 1960s saw an acceleration in the changes which have resulted in the modern-day Andalucía: urban and industrial growth, the modernisation of agriculture and the meteoric growth of tourism. Following the advent of democracy in Spain in 1982, Andalucía became an Autonomous Community with its own parliament. In 1992, when the Universal Exhibition was held in Seville, the region presented itself as a completely modern, vibrant and contemporary one.

The Straits of Gibraltar, with Africa in the background ▶

Huelva
Dunes, beaches and mountains

The westernmost province of Andalucía, located near Seville and the frontier with Portugal, the Atlantic and the Sierra Morena, is a treasure trove of surprises with regard to its historical and natural richness, still little known to tourists and travellers.

Sunset in Doñana ▸

The Doñana National Park

One of the great legends of nature conservation in Europe, the park was created in 1969 and declared Patrimony of Humanity in 1994. It runs from the right bank of the River Guadalquivir to the point where the river flows out into the Atlantic between Almonte and Sanlúcar de Barrameda. **Doñana** was the hunting estate of the Dukes of Medina Sidonia – its name derives from that of the Duchess, Doña Ana de Mendoza who retired to the modest palace inside the estate – and it was frequented by kings and other celebrated figures.

The **National Park** covers 50,720 hectares, with a further 57,000 acting as an addition protective belt. The extraordinary variety of its ecosystems and its abundant diversity of species, particularly migrating birds, make it unique among natural habitats in Europe. It covers coastal areas of shifting and stable sand dunes, pine woods, holm-oak forest, low mountains and vast horizons of dunes and lakes which hundreds of thousands of aquatic birds flock to in winter, including geese, herons, spoonbills and flamingos. Doñana is also the refuge for some particularly threatened indigenous species, such as the Iberian Lynx and the Imperial Eagle, the emblems of the Park.

Doñana ▲
Path through the dunes (above) ▶
Bird-watching point (below)

There are various visitor centres on the edge of the park which provide information, signposted routes and observatories. These are El Acebuche, La Rocina and El Acebrón near Almonte, Cerrado Garrido near Seville and Bajo de Guía in Sanlúcar de Barrameda.

The Rocío, Almonte and El Condado

Opposite Doñana is the **village of El Rocío**, with its unpaved streets. This village grew around the Hermitage of the Virgin of the Rocío and in late May or early June, at the height of spring, it is the focus for the most popular and crowded religious pilgrimage in Andalucía. Up to one million pilgrims, grouped into religious confraternities, arrive here on horseback, in carriage and carts, on foot and in every sort of vehicle in an atmosphere of celebration and dancing which reaches its peak on Whit Monday, when "The Queen of the Dunes" is brought out of the sanctuary in a packed procession.

A few kilometres away is **Almonte**, surrounded by the vineyards which cover the region of El Condado, the centre for a production of local wines produced in the village and in the nearby towns of Bollullos and La Palma. **Niebla**, the principal town of this area in the past, has a fine old cen-

The Blanca Paloma

Andalucian society's roots in the countryside manifest themselves in the Rocío pilgrimage, during which thousands of people enjoy an experience that brings them into close contact with nature for a few days. The festival's origins date back to the late 13th century, when a shepherd found a miraculous image of the Virgin on this spot, later commemorated by the construction of a hermitage. Some experts have related the devotional cult of the Virgen del Rocío, known as the Paloma Blanca (White Dove) with the survival of ancient cults of the Mother Goddess of fertility.

The Rocío pilgrimage ▲
The Rocío procession ▶

tre surrounded by Arab walls (12th century), the fortress of the Guzman (15th century), and a church that was formerly a mosque, as well as a Roman bridge over the reddish waters of the River Tinto.

Lands of Columbus

The monastery of La Rábida, Palos de la Frontera and Moguer, next to the Tinto estuary, provide the historic backdrop for Christopher Columbus's departure that led to the discovery of America in 1492. Columbus stayed in **La Rábida**, a Franciscan monastery built in the Gothic-Mudéjar style (15th century), and gained the support of the monks in his campaign to convince the Catholic Kings to fund his expedition. At his feet was the Harbour of Las Carabelas, where there are now three replicas of his ships. The church of San Jorge and other spots in **Palos de la Frontera** (in former times an active port, now an agricultural town) conjure up the place from where Columbus set sail. It was here that he recruited his crew, as well as in nearby **Moguer**, the birthplace of the poet Juan Ramón Jiménez, winner of the Nobel Prize for Literature in 1956. His house is now a Museum, while also worth noting is the convent of Santa Clara.

Church of San Jorge, Palos de la Frontera (above) ▶
Monastery of la Rábida (below)
La Fontanilla in Palos de la Frontera (above) ▼
Mudéjar cloister, monastery of la Rábida (below)

Huelva. Dunes, beaches and mountains

Convent of Santa Clara, Moguer (above) ▲
Santa María de la Granada, Moguer (left)
Monument to Juan Ramón Jiménez, Moguer (right)
Santa Clara de Moguer ▶

Huelva

The province's capital grew up on the spit of land on the estuary of the rivers Tinto and Odiel. Oriented towards the sea and towards trade, fishing and industry, Huelva now has a basically modern appearance. At its heart is the **Plaza de las Monjas** (Square of the Nuns) and the main shopping street is the **Calle Concepción**. Nearby are fine buildings such as the oldest church, San Pedro (14th-18th centuries), the **Cathedral of the Merced** (18th-century), and the Hermitage of La Cinta, located on a hill top.

The Gran Vía and the Avenida Sundheim lead to the **Huelva Museum**. Its display offers a survey starting with ancient Onuba in the first millennium before Christ to the 20th century, taking in remarkable objects such as the group of Tartessic bronzes, Greek ceramics, a Roman water-wheel from Riotinto and work by the painter Daniel Vázquez Díaz. Reminders of the British, who worked the Riotinto mines and transported minerals from the port of Huelva, are to be found in the Reina Victoria quarter of the city, whose architecture is typically English, and in the striking iron structure of the Riotinto Company Wharf, completed in 1876. Downriver from the city is a huge **monument to Columbus** measuring 37 metres high, erected at Punta del Sebo in 1929.

The Mysteries of Tartessus

Biblical and classical texts abound in references to the mythical kingdom of Tartessus, a wealthy society that practised livestock keeping and mining and where King Solomon acquired the silver to ornament his temple in Jerusalem. Despite archaeologists' efforts, its precise location is unknown, and it is uncertain if there was a great city of this name or a region with numerous settlements. One of the most likely areas for these settlements would be the Huelva Estuary, where Tartessic, Phoenician and Greek remains have been found.

Huelva ▲
Huelva Cathedral ▶

Ayamonte ▲
Isla Cristina ▶

The Costa de la Luz (Coast of Light)

Huelva's luminous Atlantic front runs along the beaches of fine sands with their dunes and pine woods which have largely retained their natural beauty. An uninterrupted 50 km stretch of beach extends to the west of the city from Mazagón and Matalascañas to Doñana. To the east, fishing and tourist centres such as Punta Umbria, La Antilla, Isla Cristina, Isla Canela alternate with stretches of sand as far as the border city of **Ayamonte**. From its colonial streets the visitor can look at the Portuguese bank of the Guadiana, reached by the bridge that has joined Andalucía and the Algarve since 1991.

The Riotinto Mines

Halfway between the coast and the mountains is the **Riotinto** exploitation, the heart of the mining activities which created the legendary fame of the Kingdom of Tartessus. Worked for 5,000 years, these mines are among the oldest in the world. The Romans worked them extensively, while from 1873 they were managed by the British Riotinto Company, which started open-cast mining. The result is obvious: huge holes in the ground such as the

Corta Atalaya, 335 metres deep and more than 1 kilometre wide, while an entire village was relocated and rebuilt after the earlier one was blown up to make way for the mining work. The English also built the exclusive Bella Vista quarter of with its Victorian buildings, as well as founding the Riotinto and Huelva football clubs, the first in Spain. The Mining Museum looks back at this history and offers a day trip on the mine train into one of the most extraordinary landscapes imaginable.

The Sierra de Aracena

The greenness of the sierra to the north of Huelva contradicts the idea of Andalucía as a dry region. Watered by crystal streams, oak woods and chestnuts cover this leafy terrain, which has been declared a natural park. On its grasslands lives the authentic Iberian pig, whose oak-fed hams are one of the stars of Andalucían cuisine. **Aracena**, the capital of the sierra, is built around a hill with a castle of a rather unusual type. Inside is the astonishing Grotto of Wonders, a fantastical labyrinth comprising 2 kilometres of caves, lakes, stalactites and stalagmites. Equally interesting are the nearby towns: Alájar, at the foot of an impressive peak; and Almonaster, with a 10th-century Arabic mosque; and Jabugo, the most famous of the ham producing centres.

Black Leg Ham

"Pata Negra" or Black Leg is the description popularly used for the finest acorn-fed Spanish ham, the gastronomic speciality of the Sierra de Huelva. This succulent leg from the indigenous Iberian pig usually has a very dark hoof and skin and weighs between 6 and 8 kilos. Cured in cool, shady rooms for between 18 and 22 months, it is highly prized for its flavourful meat that is streaked with fine veins of fat.

Valdelarco (above) ▲
Cerdo Ibérico (below) ▶
Cortegana (above) ▶▶
Riotinto (below)

Seville
A world-famous name

1. Cathedral and the Giralda
2. Real Alcázar
3. Archive of the Indies
4. Hospital de los Venerables
5. Casa de Pilatos
6. Convent of San Leandro
7. Town Hall
8. Church of the Salvador
9. Church of San Pedro
10. Fine Arts Museum
11. Convent of Santa Paula
12. Church of San Luis
13. Church of San Lorenzo
    and Basilica of the Gran Poder
14. Walls of the Macarena
15. Basilica of the Macarena
16. Regional Parliament of Andalucía
17. Torre del Oro
18. Hospital de la Caridad
19. Maestranza Bullring
20. University, Tabacco Factory
21. San Telmo Palace
22. Plaza de España
23. Plaza de América, Archaeological
    Museum and Museum of Folk Art
    and Traditions
24. Church of Santa Ana
25. Monastery of Santa María
    de las Cuevas

Capital of the Autonomous Community and the fourth largest city in Spain, Seville and its province are located on the flat plain created by the Guadalquivir as it broadens out before it reaches the sea. Ancient, historic, grand, for many its name conjures up many of the outstanding qualities of the region of Andalucía.

Seville

Located on the banks of the "great river" of Andalucía, the city's origins date back to Phoenician and Tartessic times when *Hispalis*, the early Seville, arose where land and sea met. It gained in importance, becoming one of the leading urban settlements in Spain, reaching moments of real splendour under Muslim rule. Conquered in 1248 by Ferdinand III "The Saint", the discovery of the New World brought the city immense wealth and prosperity. In the 19th century a process of urban expansion started that has accelerated up to the present day, encouraged by the international exhibitions held in 1929 and 1992. Fusing past and present, Seville has maintained its traditions into the modern age, the most important of which is Holy Week and the April Fair, two spring festivals that have brought the city so much renown.

The historic centre

Seville's historic centre, one of the largest in Europe, falls within the area bordered by the Medieval walls of the city. The most important part of this old centre is located towards the south, in the area near the river. This includes monuments declared Patrimony of Humanity in 1987: the **Cathedral**, the Alcázar (fortress) and the Archive of the Indies. The Cathedral

The Cathedral ▶
Saints Justa and Rufina by Murillo ▼

was built from 1402 onwards over the great Almohad mosque of the late 12th century. The intention of the Cathedral Chapter was to create "a work such that those who see it will take us for mad". The result was the largest Gothic church in existence, completed in 1507. Later interventions incorporated elements in classical styles. The interior has extraordinarily important objects and works of art: altarpieces, tombs of kings and illustrious figures such as Saint Ferdinand and Christopher Columbus, paintings by Zurbarán, Murillo and Goya, as well as a treasury of marvellous goldsmiths' work. Surviving from the Arabic mosque is the **Courtyard of the Orange Trees** and the tower of the **Giralda**, completed as a tower from which to call the Muslim faithful to prayer in 1198. In 1568, the element with the Renaissance bell tower was added with the weathervane of the Giraldillo, a figure personifying Faith. Standing 95 metres high, the tower is a perfect example of cultural fusion and the symbol of Seville. The Plaza del Triunfo (Square of Triumph) separates the Cathedral from the **Real Alcázar** (Royal Fortress), the monarchs' residence. This architectural complex features walls, palaces and gardens, laid out from the end of the 10th century to the 19th. Almohad doorways, the Gothic palace of Alfonso X (13th century) and various auxiliary buildings are all grouped around the Palace of Pedro I, a masterpiece of Mudéjar art completed in

The Giraldillo

The tower of the Giralda takes its name from the weather vane that tops it in the form of a huge bronze statue of Victorious Faith. This is popularly known as the Giralda or Giraldillo (meaning weather vane in Spanish), and in the past was also referred to as the Giantess or Saint Joan. It stands more than 3.5 metres high, weighs 1,500 kilos and was cast by Bartolomé Morel who completed it in 1568.

The Conception doorway (left) ▲
Interior of the Cathedral (right)
The Royal Chapel of the Cathedral ▶

1366. It features the two courtyards of La Montería and Las Doncellas and the sumptuous Salón de Embajadores (Reception Room of the Ambassadors). In front of the Alcázar is the **Archive of the Indies**, a building begun in 1583 to a design by Juan de Herrera, and which contains the most important historical archive relating to the history of South America. These monuments are complemented by the charming narrow streets and alleys of the **Barrio de Santa Cruz**, the former Jewish quarter, and typical of picturesque Seville. The perfume of orange blossom invades the small squares and narrow streets which zig-zag between courtyards and handsome buildings such as the **Hospital de los Venerables** (17th century) as well as excellent restaurants. This complex of streets runs to the **Casa de Pilatos** (House of Pilate; 16th century), a mansion which fuses the Mudéjar, Gothic and Renaissance styles.

The centre and the various barrios

The Avenida de la Constitución runs from the Cathedral to the **Town Hall** (16th and 19th centuries), located between the Plaza Nueva and the Plaza de San Francisco, two squares that must be visited. From here runs the pedestrian **Calle Sierpes**, one of the busiest which terminates in the

Courtyard of the Alcázar (left) ▲
The Episcopal Palace (right)
The Alcázar and the Santa Cruz quarter (above) ▶
The Archive of the Indies (below)

A courtyard in Seville (above) ▲
Casa de Pilatos (below)
The Santa Cruz quarter ▶

intersection of La Campana with its numerous shops. This area has numerous interesting features, such as the church of the Salvador (17th century, with the courtyard of a former mosque) which embellishes one of the most atmospheric of the city's plazas; and the parish church of the Magdalena (14th-17th centuries), where the first tribunal of the Spanish Inquisition was held in 1480. Close by is the **Museo de Bellas Artes** (Fine Arts Museum), housed in the former monastery of the Merced, dating from the 17th century. The most important area of the collection, which runs from the Middle Ages to the 20th century, is that devoted to Spanish Baroque painting, with major works by Zurbarán, Murillo, Valdés Leal and other leading names.

From the centre northwards are the other barrios of the old town centre. These include the prosperous quarters of San Vicente and San Lorenzo, with the church of Jesús del Gran Poder, a key image in Holy Week processions in Seville. The humbler barrios are those around the Mudéjar parish churches of San Pedro (where Velázquez was baptised), Santa Catalina, San Marcos and the Monastery of Santa Paula, and those around the Calles Feria and San Luis and the Alameda de Hércules. The north of the old centre is bordered by the walls of the Macarena, the most famous section of the 7km of walls that were built by the Arabs in the 12th century. Here we find the church of the Virgin of the **Macarena** and the Renaissance façade of the Parliament of Andalucía, the former Hospital de las Cinco Llagas (Hospital of the Five Wounds; 16th century).

The River and the Park

The Paseo de Colón is Seville's river frontage. It begins with the **Torre del Oro** (Tower of Gold), the defence tower built in 1221 by the Almohad dynasty to protect the original port of the city. Its name is said to derive from the gold tiles that originally covered it, or possibly the treasures that it guarded within. Juan Sebastián Elcano completed the first voyage around the world in 1522 having started out from its quayside. The Tower now houses an interesting naval museum. A garden with palm trees lies in front of the **Hospital de la Caridad** (Hospital of Charity), located in the Atarazanas – the medieval boat-building yards. Miguel de Mañara, the knight whose action-filled biography inspired the figure of Don Juan, promoted the construction this extraordinary 17th-century Baroque building which now exhibits masterpieces by Murillo and Valdés Leal's two dramatic and moving paintings on the theme of the transience of life. A few feet away lie the **Theatre** (1991) and the **Maestranza Bullring** which introduces a breath of the

The Guadalquivir and the Torre del Oro ▶

countryside into the city. This fine ring, a true "temple" of bull-fighting, was started in 1754. It is definitely worth visiting the front rows of seats and the bullfighting museum inside.

To the south of the Jerez Gateway is a planted-out area, as well as buildings such as the old **Tabacco Factory** (18th century), famous for its associations with Carmen, and the **San Telmo Palace** (17th century), the headquarters of the regional government. Built over the gardens of this palace is the **María Luisa Park**, named after the Infanta who donated the land to the city, enlivened by the unusual buildings installed at the time of the Ibero-American Exhibition of 1929. Another striking construction is Aníbal González's hemicycle known as the **Plaza de España**, built by this architect who specialised in a regional style. His Plaza de América is another fine design, flanked by the Mudéjar Pavilion that now houses the **Museum of Popular Arts and Customs**, and by the **Archaeological Museum**, which displays objects such as the Tartessic Treasure of Carambolo and the series of Roman sculptures from Itálica.

Triana and La Cartuja

On the right bank of the Guadalquivir lies the **barrio of Triana**, closely associated over the centuries with the sea,

The Carmen Legend

Some particular spots in Seville such as the Tobacco Factory and the Bullring are for ever associated with the adventures of a fictitious character who has become a universally known legend: Carmen, symbol of liberty and female passions. Created by the French writer Prosper Mérimée in a short story published in 1845, she acquired world fame when George Bizet's opera of the same title was first performed in Paris in 1875.

Bullring of the Real Maestranza ▲
The Tobacco Factory, now the University (above) ▶
Plaza de España (below)

with flamenco and with bullfighting. The Isabel II iron bridge (dating from 1852 and the first fixed iron bridge in the city) leads into the typical Altozano Square. The Calle Betis starts here, running along a charming line of coloured houses reflected in the river. Behind is the corner with the Calle Pureza and the church of Santa Ana, one of the oldest in the city, founded in 1276. The route continues up the streets known as Castille and Alfarería which have numerous workshops producing the ceramics typical of Triana, as well as bars where the visitor can enjoy a tapa or two.

The **Isla de la Cartuja** (Island of the Carthusian Monastery) adds a modern note. This large area between offshoots of the Guadalquivir was the venue for the 1992 Universal Exhibition, and has since then been an amusement park. The Carthusian monastery survives among the recently-created avenues and modern buildings and is now a cultural centre. It was founded in 1400 and converted into a ceramics factory in the 19th century. Along the river we see the bridges built to connect with the other bank for the Exhibition: notable among these is the Alamillo, standing 130 metres high, designed by Santiago Calatrava and often used as the emblem of the new, modernised Seville.

Exhibitions in Seville
The history of 20th-century Seville was marked by two major exhibitions which were important for the city's modernisation. In 1929 the Spanish-South American exhibition helped to launch an updated vision of Seville, which became in important tourist destination from then on. The Universal Exhibition in 1992 added a contemporary dimension and resulted in the updating of its infrastructures with the arrival of the High Speed Train known as the "AVE" from Madrid and the construction of new bridges over the Guadalquivir, among other innovations.

Expo 92 ▲

Holy Week in Seville ▶

Around the city

Around 9 kms north of Seville are the ruins of **Itálica**, the Roman city founded by Scipio in the year 206 BC. It was the birthplace of both Trajan and Hadrian, the latter responsible for its apogee in the 2nd century AD. The remains feature luxurious villas with courtyards and mosaics, a theatre, temples, baths and a huge amphitheatre, one of the largest in the Empire. To the west of Seville is the plain of the Alijarafe. Set among olive trees, vines and estates are 20 or so villages that offer the ideal venue for a rural break from the city. The Sierra Norte (Northern Range) covers the northern strip of the province, with a landscape of grassland and woods, now categorised as national park. In the centre of the sierra (around 90 kms from Seville) are the towns of Cazalla de la Sierra and Constantina, with their attractive town centres, offering fine locally-made liqueur and cured meats.

Carmona

To the east of Seville (35 kms) is **Carmona**, located high up on a ridge with the river valley at its feet. Few towns have such a well-preserved, atmospheric old centre. On the outskirts is a remarkable 1st-4th century Roman necropolis

House of the Birds, Itálica ▶
Mosaic of the Planets, Itálica (below)
Constantina (above and below) ▼

which has been excavated. The church of San Pedro and its tower known as the Giraldilla are particularly notable, along with the Puerta de Sevilla Arabic fortress which marks the entrance to the old walled town.

Towns and villages near Seville

Culturally and artistically, the area around Seville is one of the richest in all of Andalucía. It features large, tranquil and friendly villages and small towns that house a wealth of architectural styles and constructions, particularly of the Baroque period, as well as works of art. In a radius of 100 kms from Seville we find **Écija**, with its numerous Baroque bell-towers and a wealth of outstanding religious buildings and town palaces; **Marchena**, with its Islamic fortress, and the church of San Juan, and a museum of sculpture; **Osuna**, a ducal town, its streets adorned with palaces presided over by the majestic Church. Estepa, Morón, Utrera, Alcalá de Guadaira and other interesting towns and village offer further possibilities.

Church of S. Pedro and Alcázar de la Puerta Sevilla, Carmona (above) ▶▶
Collegiate church, Osuna (below)
Church of Santa María, Écija (above) ▶
Arco de la Rosa, Marchena (below) ▼
Carmona, pages 46-47

Cádiz
Wine and the ocean

The province of Cádiz looks towards the sea. Its unique light, its location, cities, people and even its wines reflect its leading role in the south of Europe on the western edge of the Mediterranean and extremely close to North Africa.

Sunset, Cádiz ▶

Sanlúcar de Barrameda

Located on the mouth of the Guadalquivir, opposite Doñana, **Sanlúcar de Barrameda** is a happy combination of coast and countryside. This is where Manzanilla is made, a delicate, light drink with a tang of the sea. A "sacred place" for sailors, it was among the first ports in Andalucía and one of the most select holiday destinations from the 19th century onwards, a past still evident in traditions such as the horse race held on the sands every summer since 1845. Divided in two by a steep hill, the Upper Town has the Castle of Santiago, the Mudéjar Church of La O and the palaces of the Dukes of Medina Sidonia and the Dukes of Orleans. In the Lower Town, a network of long straight streets runs from the Plaza del Cabildo to the seashore and the Bajo de Guía, with its famous seafood and fish restaurants.

Jerez de la Frontera

This great city in Lower Andalucía is a centre of wine production, horse breeding and flamenco. Jerez rises up among the chalk coloured slopes of the vineyards that extend into the far distance. It is an ancient place, one of the defensive positions on the frontier with the kingdom of

Castle of Santiago, Sanlúcar (above) ▲
The fish market (below)
Church of Desamparados, Sanlúcar (above) ▶
Bodegas Barbadillo, Sanlúcar (below)

Granada. Its centre is focused around the Medieval castle, surrounded by wide avenues, parks and wineries. The 12th-13th-century **Alcázar** (Arab Fortress) reminds us of the period of Islamic rule, with its mosque now consecrated as a Christian church, its Arabic baths, palaces and gardens. To its side is the **Cathedral** (17th-18th-century), crowned by a 40 metre diameter dome. It houses outstanding works of art including a canvas by Zurbáran. The traditional September grape-treading festival takes place in front of the Cathedral. The visitor gains a feeling of the oldest part of the city in the plazas of the Asunción (Assumption) and Plateros (Silversmiths), the church of San Dionisio (13th-15th centuries), the Cabildo Viejo (16th-century), and a cluster of parish churches including San Miguel, San Mateo, San Lucas, as well as typical town palaces.

The modern part of the city runs along the Arenal, the Calle Larga and the surrounding streets. In contrast, the typical flamenco quarter is focused on the gypsy barrio of Santiago, where great performers have kept alive the tradition of the type of singing known as "cante jondo". Jerez's role as a centre of wine production is evident in the "cathedrals of wine" represented by its bodegas or wineries (many open to the public). Their great dark aisles old

The Carthusian monastery at Jérez (above) ▲
The Royal Andalucián Equestrian School (below)
Jérez Cathedral ▶

the barrels of fermenting sherries: amontillados, olorosos, Pedro Ximénez, famous around the world. The Archaeological Museum and the Clock Museum are also worth visiting, as is the Recreo de las Cadenas which houses the **Royal Equestrian School of Andalucia** where thoroughbreed Andalucían horses perform. On the outskirts of the city is the fine **Cartuja** (Carthusian Monastery), which features Gothic, Renaissance and Baroque elements. The Race Track is the venue for motorcycle racing.

El Puerto de Santa María

The other side of the wine triangle lies on **El Puerto de Santa María,** located next to the mouth of the Guadalete and the Bay of Cadiz. Lying on the axis of the town's regular ground-plan are the Castle of San Marcos, built after the Christian Reconquest over a 10th-century Islamic oratory, and the Gothic tracery of the Priory Church. These streets, where the poet Rafael Alberti spent his childhood, offer the traditional pleasures of life in this part of Andalucía, from the renowned Bullring, to a stroll along the Ribera del Guadalete with its bustling bars and terrace restaurants serving the finest seafood.

Bodega la Mezquita, Jerez (above) ▲
El Puerto de Santa María (below)
The Priorate church, El Puerto de Santa María ▶

Puerta de Tierra ▲
Campo del Sur. Cathedral ▶
Towers and terraces, Cadiz, pages 58-59

Cadiz

The most ancient city in Europe is suspended in the Atlantic itself, only joined to the mainland by a sandy strip and by the bridge over the Bay. Gades, founded according to myth by Hercules himself, but in reality by the Phoenicians around 1100 BC, was a wealthy trading centre in Antiquity and the last outpost of the Mediterranean civilisation. The discovery of South America changed its fate: a cross road between oceans and continents, Cadiz became the departure and arrival point for the fleets, and in 1717 the colonial metropolis. In the 19th century the city was the basis for Spain's liberal reform movement, and the first Spanish Constitution was pronounced here in 1812.

The modern part of the city and the Playa de la Victoria run as far as the **Puertas de Tierra** (Land Gates), the only land entrance to the city. They form part of the impenetrable defensive ring built to protect Cadiz in the 17th and 18th centuries after the terrible Sack of 1596. These defensive ramparts lead into the barrio of Santa María with the monastery of Santo Domingo (17th century) and to the Gateway and **Plaza of San Juan de Dios**, the centre of the old town presided over by the **Town Hall**. Nearby are the Plaza de España, with the monument to the Liberal Parliament

Manuel de Falla

The composer of *Amor Brujo*, *El Sombrero de Tres Picos* and other celebrated works is one of Cadiz's most famous personalities. De Falla was born there in 1876 but trained in Madrid and Paris. He knew Debussy, Albéniz and Ravel and was a friend of Picasso and Lorca. His work fuses the classical tradition with popular Andalucian music. De Falla died in exile in Argentina in 1946, after the Spanish Civil War.

(Cortes) of 1812, and, on the Calle Rosario, the wonderful little oratorio of the Santa Cueva (Holy Cave) with its dome painted by Goya. Behind San Juan de Dios wind the narrow streets of the Pópulo quarter, the oldest barrio in the city, between the remains of the Roman theatre, the church-fortress of the Old Cathedral (17th century), and the Casa de la Contaduría (Cathedral Museum). Rising above the colourful façades and the breakwater of the Campo del Sur is the hemispherical tiled dome of the new **Cathedral**, the great church funded by trade with South America and built between 1722 and 1883.

Beyond the Cathedral is the tapestry of streets formed by Columela, Ancha, San José and Sagasta. From the Tavira Tower (open to the public and with a fascinating "camera obscura" inside offering a 360 degree projected view of the city) one looks over the entire city and the remarkable landscape of watchtowers which were built so that merchants could see their ships arriving in port. In a nearby small square is the **Oratorio of San Felipe Neri** whose chapel has a fine *Immaculate Virgin* by Murillo. This was the meeting point for the constitutional Parliament or Cortes, the subject of the adjacent museum. Nearby are the 18th-century Women's Hospital, an example of local Baroque architecture with a painting by El Greco; the Gran Teatro Falla, the venue for the carnival competitions; and one street away, the Plaza de San Antonio and the charming **Plaza de Mina**. Here we find the **Cadiz Museum**, whose archaeological exhibits are witness to the huge riches lying beneath the ground level of this city. Among the objects and works of art on display are a pair of male and female sarcophagi from the Near East dating from the 5th century BC, and a series of oil paintings by Zurbarán. From the Plaza de Mina we reach the Alameda de Apodaca and the outer ring of the old town which faces the sea. This takes us from the colonial style façade of the Carmelite church to the **Castle of Santa Catalina**, designed in 1598, the oldest surviving building in the city. Next to it is the start of the popular beach of La Caleta and alongside it the typical picturesque barrios such as **La Viña** with its church of La Palma, to the Market and the **Plaza de las Flores** near the Cathedral. Here we find the fullest expression of the character and cheerful nature of the people of Cadiz, expressed to its fullest in the famous Carnival.

From Medina Sidonia to Tarifa

To the south of Cadiz we turn inland following the "route of the bull" to a region of live-stock ranches, or we stick to the coast road and follow the wonderful shoreline all the way to Gibraltar. **Medina Sidonia** surveys the countryside from the top of a hill. The ancient Asido, at it was called by the

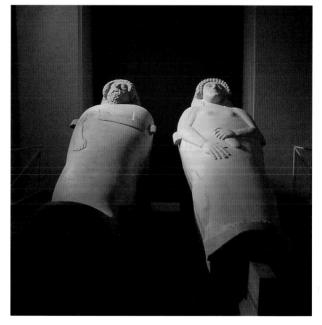

Cadiz Town Hall (above) ▲
Phoenician sarcophagi (below)
Cathedral (above) ▶
Plaza de las Flores (below)

Church of Santa María la Coronada, Medina Sidonia ▲

Medina Sidonia ▶

Phoenicians, Romans and Muslims, was the power base for the dukes of Medina Sidonia, among the leading aristocrats in Spain. Its grand town centre reflects this pass. The Pastora Arch, the Muslim entrance to the city, leads to the old town, which climbs up to the church of Santa María la Coronada (Saint Mary the Crowned; 15th-16th centuries). Looking towards the mountains in the distance we can make out **Alcalá de los Gazules**, whose main feature is the Plaza Alta (Upper Square) with the church of San Jorge (15th century) and the Casa del Cabildo (Town Hall) now the information office for the **natural park of Alcornocales**. This extends over 170,000 hectares in the nearby mountains and is one of the best preserved and largest expanses of Mediterranean forest.

The coast to the south of Cadiz

Vejer de la Frontera rises up like a lighthouse with the sea in front of it. Its winding old town centre, typical of the Muslim style, creates a network of alleys and passages of white buildings. It also has ancient walls, the church of the Saviour, monasteries and mansions. At the foot of the town is the great Atlantic coast. Towards Cadiz lie the bays of **Conil**, the castle of Sancti Petri and **Chiclana de la Frontera**. Towards Tarifa are the beaches of Cape Trafalgar and **Barbate**, the latter a fishing village with a huge beach that runs to **Zahara de los Atunes**. Even more delightful is Bolonia, the magical cove with a huge sand dune and the ruins of a Roman city. A group of wind generators herald the approach to **Tarifa**, the most southerly point of Europe and a paradise for winds and for surfing. Colonised by the Phoenicians, this was the first place in the Peninsular where the Muslims set foot in 710AD, naming it after their leader Tarif. Still standing are the cities walls and castle built by Abderramán III in the year 960 and where Guzmán the Good made the heroic gesture of sacrificing his son rather than surrendering. From its ramparts we can see the coast of Africa, so close that it seems possible to reach out and touch it. The Cadiz coastline runs as far as the **Straits of Gibraltar** and the great port city of **Algeciras**, with its bay running round to Gibraltar. The Mediterranean starts with the luxurious residential complexes of Soto Grande.

Tarifa (above) ▶
Ruins at Bolonia (below)
Beach at Valdevaqueros, Tarifa (above) ▼
Vejer de la Frontera (below)

Gibraltar

One of the most notable features on the southern flank of Andalucia is the Rock of Gibraltar. Conquered in 1704 during the War of Spanish Succession by an Anglo-Dutch fleet, it became a British territory as a consequence of the Treaty of Utrecht in 1713. Despite numerous attempts to recapture it throughout the 18th century, it is still a colony, whose British character contrasts strongly with Andalucian villages and towns nearby.

Arcos and Ronda
Romantic mountains

Mid-way between the provinces of Cádiz and Malaga we find a range of mountains in which the beauty of the landscape blends with the traditional charm of its whitewashed villages. This is the romantic region that runs between Arcos and Ronda, the "route of the White Villages".

Ronda ▶

Arcos de la Frontera

Arcos has been described as the most beautiful city in Spain, and the archetype of an Andalucian village: raised up on the crown of a peak next to the River Guadalete, Arcos de la Frontera is a cascade of white houses dotted with church towers and walls. Of Roman and Arabic origins, it acquired its character in the Middle Ages when it became a frontier fortress at the gates of the Muslim kingdom of Granada. The visitor climbs up the Cuesta de Belén through the charming Upper Town in an intricate network of narrow streets, walls and little squares all expressive of the natural elegance of this type of architecture with its whitewashed walls, wrought-iron grilles and courtyards filled with flowers. At the top is a panoramic viewpoint suspended over a breathtaking gorge, next to the castle, a former Islamic fortress. Above the rooftops rise the bell towers of the churches of **Santa María de la Asunción** (15th-18th centuries), a blend of Gothic, Mudéjar and Baroque, filled with works of arts and interesting legends, and **San Pedro**, also impressive and similarly worth visiting for its works of art.

Church of Santa María ▲
Parador hotel ▶

The Pueblos Blancos (White Villages)

From Arcos on the Sierra de Cadiz starts to appear, linking up with the Sierra de Ronda. Here we find the traditional white, picturesque villages that adorn this rocky, wooded sierra, located along the roads that run towards Ronda. Between hills in the Guadalete Valley are **Bornos** and **Algodonales**, and in the distance the eagle's nest of **Zahara**, redolent of Romantic frontier tales, set at the foot of an Arabic castle. Similarly located and presiding over a landscape of hills and olive groves is **Olvera**, whose fine outline is accentuated by its medieval castle and the Neoclassical church of the Incarnation. An unusual villages is **Setenil de las Bodegas** which may surprise the visitor. Rather than opting for an elevated location, its streets are buried in the twists and turns of a gorge, beneath huge rocky outcrops. Its name is said to derive from the Latin *septem nihil* – seven times nothing – after the Christians' seven failed attempts to recapture it before its conquest in 1484.

Sierra de Cádiz ▲
Olvera ▶

The Sierra de Grazalema

The **Sierra de Grazalema** is the heart of the Pueblos Blancos. Categorised as a Biospheric Nature Reserve and a **Natural Park**, it covers 50,000 hectares and is a unique area. The large amount of rainfall – at times this is the wettest place in Spain – the dramatic limestone crags and the dense woodland all create one of the most striking landscapes in Andalucía. In addition there is a very interesting range of wildlife and plants that flourish in Mediterranean wet zones, with various types of oaks and the rare *Abies pinsapo*, a type of fir tree left over the glacial period in Europe and now confined to the mountains of Cadiz and Ronda.

The clean-cut architecture of El Bosque, which acts as the entrance too the Park, as well as Benamahoma, Villaluenga, Benaocaz and other small villages with a Moorish atmosphere are dotted around the hills and valleys of this area. Located among the peaks is **Ubrique**, the largest town in the sierra, and famous for its leather-craft, as well as **Grazalema**, a typical mountain town. Its old centre has cobbled streets where fountains splash water in the shade of cypress and fir trees. An oasis of peace and pure air at 830 metres above sea level.

Ubrique (above) ▲
Leather workshop (below)
Grazalema ▶

Ronda

Moving eastwards into the province of Malaga is **Ronda**, the capital of the sierra and a town which has rightly been the subject of enormous interest and admiration over the centuries. The beauty of this "ideal city" of poets and travellers is difficult to convey in words. It lies on a rocky outcrop above a vertical precipice whose cliff falls down 180 metres. Ronda creates a dream-like sensation seen from a distance, an impression confirmed once inside the city that for many epitomises the Andalucía of the Romantic writers and travellers, land of bullfighters and bandits in which legend and history fuse, echoed by the drama of the landscape.

The Guadalavín gorge divides Ronda into two. On one side is the part known as the Ciudad (City), the old Medieval area, and on the other the Mercadillo. They are joined by the **Puente Nuevo** (New Bridge), a dizzying structure completed in 1793. The **Ciudad** falls within the Muslim walls when the "fortress" of Ronda was a court of one of the Arab kingdoms and the best defended frontier outpost of the Kingdom of Granada. The Arab princes were succeeded by Christian knights following the Reconquest by the Catholic Kings in 1485. This aristocratic feel pervades the old town, with its turrets and walls, churches, monasteries and town palaces.

Arch of Philip V (left) ▲
Principal church (right)
La Mina (below)
Puente Nuevo, Ronda ▶

Particularly notable is the **Church of the Incarnation**, on a cathedral-like scale and built over the main Mosque in the 16th and 17th centuries. **The Modragón Palace** (now the City Museum) is one of the finest and most handsome buildings in the city, with tiled courtyards and gardens that look out over the Gorge. The Museum of Banditry pays homage to legend, while the town's Islamic past is evident in the Arab Baths (13th century) and in the **Mine of the House of the Moorish King**. This is a subterranean staircase with 365 steps that descends to the bottom of the cliff.

Bullfighters of Ronda

The typically Spanish, Romantic-era spirit of Ronda is largely due to its famous bullfighters, who imbued it with the spirit of the ring, austere and valiant. The greatest of these was Pedro Romero (1754-1839), considered the inventor of modern bullfighting. Over his lengthy career he killed more than 5,600 bulls without ever being seriously wounded. Among the most famous of the modern bullfighters from Ronda is Antonio Ordóñez.

The **Mercadillo**, opposite the Ciudad, is more recent and bustling, lively part of town focused around the pedestrian street called Carrera de Espinel. Next to the Alameda del Tajo (Gorge Walkway) is the **Bullring**, a renowned ring where the Romero dynasty paved the way for modern bullfighting. This mythical place in bullfighting history, with its slim stone arcading, was opened in 1785. Every September bullfights in period dress of the time of Goya recreate the spectacle and colour of a Romantic-era event with bullfighters and the public dressed appropriately.

The Genal Valley and the Sierra de las Nieves

To the south of Ronda is the coast road, the old mountain route of mule drivers and smugglers, with the Mediterranean as its backdrop. Towards Gibraltar we cross the hidden **Genal Valley**, with its oak and chestnut woods and a cluster of small villages such as Alpandeire, Cartájima, Benalauría, Benadalid, and Algatocín heading towards **Gaucín** built beneath a crag crowned by the Castle of the Eagle. On the road down from Ronda towards the Costa del Sol is the **Sierra de las Nieves**, an important natural park with Alpine slopes and pinsapo fir trees, with the coastline of Africa visible across the water.

The Bullring at Ronda ▶

Malaga
The Costa del Sol

The province of Malaga, whose mountains curve around in parallel to the Mediterranean, has a marvellous warm, sunny climate. Malaga and the Costa del Sol are wonderful parts of Andalucía, the most oriented towards tourism, the most cosmopolitan and the most famous parts of the region internationally.

Malaga ▶

The western Costa del Sol

The western coastline of Malaga is the heart of the Costa del Sol, the region's main tourist zone. It forms a continuous shoreline of cities, housing developments, hotel complexes and leisure facilities that have grown at the feet of mountain ranges dotted with white villages, the "pueblos blancos". The Malaga coastline starts with the beaches of **Manilva** and **Casares**, whose urban centres are inland, between crags on which the whitewashed villages are located, creating a typical image of an Andalucian village. **Estepona**, which arises from the foothills of the Sierra Bermeja, spreads out from the centre of the Plaza de las Flores and the Church of the Remedios (18th century), down to the port and the Paseo Maritimo, the beaches with their old watch towers and the surrounding area with numerous golf courses and housing developments.

Marbella

The show case for luxury tourism, and famed for its international jet set, it offers the luxury and leisure facilities for which the Costa del Sol is famous. This thriving tourism capital has a unique micro-climate on the coast, protected from the north winds by the Sierra Blanca. From ancient times this was a favoured spot – the Roman baths known as "las Bóvedas" are located here – while it was later a Muslim fortress and a Christian city from 1485. In the 19th century it grew and prospered from mining and industry. However, this prosperity reached new levels from the 1950s onwards when it became an elite holiday resort. This old city has now become the centre of an extended urban zone featuring various yachting harbours and a dozen or so golf courses. The heart of the old town is the Plaza de los Naranjos (Square of the Orange Trees), surrounded by the town hall, that dates from 1568, and various other old buildings. The narrow streets around it lead to the Hospital Bazán (now the Museum of Printmaking) and the parish church of the Incarnation (18th century). The apartment blocks, the large houses, and the modern mosque, all create a cosmopolitan feel. The shoreline offers a succession of fine beaches – Fontanilla, los Monteros, las Chapas, etc, while to the west is **Puerto Banús**, a centre of nightlife and the mooring-point for luxury yachts, and the busy waterside town of **San Pedro de Alcántara**. The town in the hills that lie behind Marbella and which offer a complete contrast of mood and atmosphere, include the beautiful Moorish Ojén and Istán.

Sardines and fried fish
Along with the modern, touristic side of the Costa del Sol with its golf courses, yachting marinas and luxurious residential complexes, the coast near Malaga has retained a fine culinary tradition based on excellent fish caught off its own shores. The most popular are the "espetones", sardines on wooden skewers grilled on the beach, and the mixed fried fish platters which include a wide variety of the best local species, such as anchovies and whitebait, dipped in flour and fried in olive oil.

Golf course, Marbella ▲
Casares (above) ▶
Puerto Banús (below)

From Marbella to Malaga

Sun and sand are the two factors that have resulted in the extraordinary growth of this stretch of coastline from Marbella to the capital, running through the former little fishing villages now transformed into a global Babel. From the Arab castle of Sohail (10th century) Fuengirola stretches along a Paseo Marítimo of 7 kms. On the mountains behind is **Mijas**, famous for its marble, its irregular shaped bullring, its winding streets, and its donkey-taxis. Benalmádena is divided between an old village, which offers magnificent views over the Mediterranean, and the new area around the harbour. The coast continues up to **Torremolinos**, a town which pioneered low-budget summer tourism, and the fine sandy beach of Carihuela, a medley of beach bars and restaurants which offer "fried fish", the typical Malaga dish.

Málaga

The second largest city in Andalucía, and the sixth in Spain, the city of **Malaga** lies in a river basin fed by the Guadalmedina on the banks of the Mediterranean. Traditionally open both to land and sea routes, its origins can be traced back to the 8th century BC, when the Phoenicians

Mijas (above) ▶
Fuengirola (below)
The vaults of Malaga Cathedral (above) ▼
Malaga Cathedral (below)

established the trading post of Malaka. Under the Muslims, the city became the leading port of the southern peninsula and in the 19th century it enjoyed another period of prosperity due to the wine and fruit trades. Modern Malaga continues to be a vibrant developing city, its economy based on service industries and tourism, while it has also made great efforts to retain its traditions, such as the Easter Week processions, the Fair and the Verdiales traditional festivals.

The old centre is focused around the most famous monuments that lie at the feet of the hills known as the **Gibralfaro** - the "hill of the lighthouse", fortified by the Muslims and offering the finest views of the city and the **Alcazaba**, the Islamic area laid out over Roman foundations between the 8th and 14th centuries. This has a double ring of walls and a palace area dating from the 11th century when Malaga was the court of one of the Divided Kingdoms, extended under the Nasrid dynasty in the 13th-15th centuries. At the bottom are the tiers of a surviving Roman theatre of the 1st century AD. This attractive street leads to the **Cathedral**, a monumental building nicknamed "la manquita" (the one-armed lady) as one of its twin-towers is unfinished. The building was started on the site of the old mosque in 1528 under the direction of Enrique Egas, continuing until the end of the 18th century, with the result that the Cathedral is a Gothic-Renaissance building with later Baroque features, such as the main façade in polychrome marble. Its nave and aisles, chapels and museum house a wealth of works of art, from the choirstalls with carvings by Pedro de Mena, to paintings by Luis de Morales, José de Ribera and Alonso Cano. On the plaza at the front is the Episcopal Palace (16th-18th centuries).

The narrow streets of the old town run between palaces and parish churches such as the **church of Saint James the Pilgrim**, which houses the much venerated image of Jesus el Rico, culminating in the Plaza de la Merced. One of the houses on this square was the birthplace of Pablo Picasso in 1881, and the house now houses a museum devoted to his life and work. Running up from the **Plaza de la Merced**, the calle Victoria leads to the **Sanctuario de la Victoria** or Sanctuary of the Virgin of Victory, patron saint of the city, a building dating from 1700, and from there down to the Plaza de la Constitución, with its famous and old-fashioned Pasaje de Chinitas and the pedestrian **Calle Marqués de Larios**, the main shopping street that runs down to the port. The city faces the sea with a long stretch of wide avenues planted out with trees and sub-tropical shrubs. Towards the west is the **Alameda Principal**, with the main food market and the museum of the Mesón de la Victoria behind, the river bed of the Guadalmedina and the working-class quarter of el Perchel. To the east is the Paseo del Parque with its tropical trees and the Art Nouveau-style Town Hall dating from

Picasso's birth place and museum (above) ▲
The Alcazaba (below)
The Alcazaba ▶

1919, the bullring and the area called la Malagueta. Beyond this the road continues along the front with the charming old fishing barrios of Pedregalejo and El Palo. Here the beach restaurants offer sardines on wooden sticks grilled on the beach and other typical fish dishes.

Antequera and El Torcal

On a mountain platform 50km inland from Malaga is **Antequera**, a meeting-point of roads and the geographical centre of Andalucía. This ancient city has a splendid historic centre. The outskirts offer the dolmens of Menga, Viera and El Romeral, dating back 4,500 years and considered among the finest in Europe. The upper part of town has the Arab fortress, the Collegiate Church of Santa María, completed in 1550, and interesting chapels such as the Chapel of el Portichuelo. The lower town has a proliferation of Baroque architecture, with outstanding buildings such as the Collegiate Church of San Sebastián (16th-18th centuries) and the Palace of Nájera (18th century), a museum which houses the important Roman bronze known as *The Youth of Antequera*. In addition, there are the riches of El Torcal, a fantastical labyrinth of stone forms sculpted by wind and water into strange forms.

Vélez-Málaga ▶
El Torcal de Antequera (above) ▼
The Axarquía (below)

The Axarquía and the eastern Costa del Sol

To the east of Malaga lies the Axarquía, a wooded region of vineyards and orchards, and of Muslim villages that run down to the Mediterranean under a dazzling light. **Vélez Málaga** is the capital of this idyllic area. The Moorish fortress, the church of Santa María and the Villa quarter rise up above an old centre that has some notable buildings including the parish church of San Juan (16th century). The nearby hills house the famous towns of the region, known for their wines, raisins and sugar cane: **Cómpeta**, on the slopes of the natural park of the Sierras de Alhama, Tejeda, and Almijara, **Frigiliana** with its unspoiled Moorish centre, and **Torrox**, a cluster of whitewashed houses adorned with flowers.

Nerja

The Costa del Sol runs along the coastline of the Axarquía as far as **Nerja**, which is touristy but also traditional. From the viewing-point known as the Balcón de Europa the visitor can see the cliffs and bays of the clear waters of the eastern coastline. The town centre dominated by the church of the Saviour. On the outskirts of the town an unmissable trip is the famous cave, discovered by chance in 1959.

Cómpeta (above) ▲
Nerja cave (below)
Frigiliana (above) ▶
Cliffs at Maro, Nerja (below)

Córdoba
The aristocratic centre

1. Torre de La Calahorra
2. Arab waterwheel
3. Roman Bridge
4. Mosque-Cathedral
5. Episcopal Palace
6. Alcázar of the Christian Kings
7. Arab Walls and Gateways
8. Synagogue
9. Bullfighting Museum
10. Archaeological Museum
11. Plaza del Potro
12. Fine Arts Museum and
    Julio Romero de Torres Museum
13. Plaza de la Corredera
14. Church of San Nicolás de la Villa
15. Church of Santa Marina
16. Viana Palace
17. Plaza del Cristo de los Faroles
18. Convent of the Merced

From the Sierra Morena to the rolling land of the Guadalquivir valley, the province of Córdoba covers a large area of the centre of Andalucía. The capital of the province and the ring of villages around it are a noble testimony to the historical grandeur of the region.

The Judería quarter ▲
River Guadalquivir ▶

Córdoba

Córdoba lies next to the Guadalquivir, at the foot of the Sierra Morena. With its origins dating back to Phoenician times, *Corduba* was re-founded in the 2nd century BC by the Romans, who made it the capital of the province of Bética. In the year 756 the Omeyyad prince Abderramán I established the centre of the kingdom of Al-Andalus there. It reached its peak in the 10th century as the principal city of the caliphate proclaimed by Abderramán III, at which period it was the leading city in the West, a focus of culture and tolerance in which Jews, Muslims and Christian co-existed. After the demise of the Omeyyad dynasty, the city was conquered by Ferdinand III in 1236, becoming the feudal heart of the most ancient Christian lineages. Birthplace of Seneca and Averroes, of Gongora and Julio Romero de Torres, Córdoba houses many of the keys to the soul of Andalucía within the walls of its remarkable town centre, rightly declared Patrimony of Humanity.

The Mosque and the Judería (Jewish Quarter)

The old city centre follows the lines of the Muslim medina, with its axis of the Mosque and the river. The Arab tower of the **Calahorra**, remodelled in the 14th century, has a muse-

um devoted to the three cultures (Islamic, Christian and Hebrew) that characterised the city at its greatest period, and controlled the access to the **Roman bridge**, situated on a line with the **Mosque**. On the right bank, along with the Baroque monument of the *Triumph of the Archangel Raphael*, patron saint of the city, is the impressive rectangle formed by the **Mosque-Cathedral**, one of the most remarkable of all Islamic buildings in Europe. Abderramán I began work on it in the year 785 on a site occupied by a Visigothic basilica. In 833, Abderramán II enlarged the prayer hall, and in the next century Abderramán III built a new prayer tower, while his son Alhakem II began the most important expansion, while Almanzor gave it its definitive appearance. Contrasting the sobriety of the exterior, only interrupted by a chain of delicate entrances, is the graceful perfumed vegetation and the fountains of the **Patio of the Orange Trees**, where the faithful would originally have washed themselves before prayers. On the north side of the Patio is the tower, remodelled in the classical style of the 16th and 17th centuries, and on the opposite side, the oratory. This is a space with 19 aisles of continuous two-coloured arches resting on hundreds of columns that create a unique and unforgettable sight, a forest of brick and stone that creates infinite vistas and nuances of light. In the oldest parts the capitals of the columns are

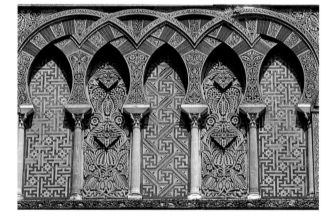

The Calahorra Tower (above) ▲
Exterior of the Mosque (below)
The Mosque (above) ▶
Courtyard of the Orange Trees (below)

Interior of the Mosque ▶
Dome of the maqsura (above) ▼
Maqsura and mihrab (below)

reused Roman and Visigothic ones. On the south wall is the *mihrab*, the niche that directs the faithful towards Mecca, covered in glinting coloured mosaics made by Byzantine craftsmen. This is preceded by the equally refined domes of the *maqsura*, the area reserved for the Caliph. The original state of the Mosque was altered in the 16th century when a Gothic-Renaissance Cathedral was built inside it. When he saw this addition, Charles V is said to have remarked: "you have made what can be found in many places, and you have spoiled what was unique in the world".

Also located next to the river is the **Alcázar of the Reyes Cristianos** (Fortress of the Christian Kings), built in 1327 by King Alfonso XI over Caliphate houses. In addition to its peaceful gardens, it has a magnificent collection of Roman objects. Extending from trom the Mosque and the Alcázar is the **Judería**, the old Jewish quarter with its labyrinthine streets, and the heart of the old city. Here, among little squares and fortified walls, are the most secret corners of the city, the little courtyards filled with pots and plants, the 14th-century **Synagogue**, one of the few to have survived in Spain, the **Bullfighting Museum**, recording the history of one of the country's most traditional customs, and of course the friendly welcome of the local inns and tapas bars.

From the old town to the centre and the outskirts

To the east of the Mosque are other nearby areas filled with interesting buildings, such as the **Archaeological Museum**, a 15th-16th-century palace which has an excellent display of Caliphate art. Near the river is the **Plaza del Potro**, located in a humble quarter mentioned by Cervantes and in which are now located the **Fine Arts Museum** (Museo de Bellas Artes) and the **Julio Romero de Torres Museum**. The latter displays the work of a painter whose chosen subject-matter was typically Andalucian, particularly his portraits and religious works. To the north lie the **Plaza de la Corredera** (17th century) which looks like a typical Castilian main, market square, and the **Plaza de las Tendillas**, the centre of Córdoba and the link to the modern city via the avenue known as Gran Capitán, as well as to the more ordinary quarters of the city. Here we find the remains of the Roman temple of Claudius Marcellus, as well as well-known parish churches such as San Nicolás de la Villa (13th-16th centuries) and Santa Marina, founded by Ferdinand III shortly after the Reconquest. Opposite is the monument to the short-lived Cordoban bullfighter Manolete, and the **Palacio de Viana** (14th-17th centuries). The palace is typical of an aristocratic mansion, with 14 interior courtyards and a wealth of works of art. Continuing on our route, we reach the plaza of **Cristo de los Faroles** (Christ of the Lanterns),

The Synagogue (above) ▲
Courtyard (below)
River Guadalquivir (above) ▶
Palace-fortress of the Christian Kings (below)

before leaving the old town by the gardens that form part of the finest example of Baroque architecture in Córdoba, the old convent of La Merced (18th century).

Around Córdoba

Only 10 kms separate Córdoba from **Medina Azahara**, the courtly city built by the Caliph Abderramán III from the year 936 onwards at the feet of the Sierra Morena. Its short-lived beauty and refinement (it was destroyed by Berber rebels in the year 1010 as the Caliphate began to decline) is still evident today in its ruins. It occupies a rectangle of rising terraces that lead up to the mosque and to living areas for 15,000 people, culminating in the palace area with its ponds, gardens and luxurious rooms. The so-called "Salón Rico" gives some idea of its past glories: horse-shoe arches, columns of different colours, pierced and carved columns, stuccoed walls and carved marbles with foliate reliefs pointing to the classical and Oriental roots of Omeyyad art. The slopes of the Sierra Morena offer a fine viewing point over the city, and **Las Ermitas** with its valley. In the distance, further to the north, is the area known as **Los Pedroches**, a region of grazing land and peaceful towns.

Córdoba, a rich larder

Cordoba is one of the richest provinces in Andalucia with regard to its agriculture. Among its most important and highly prized products are its wine and olive oil, classified by the Denominación de Origen (Denomination of Origin) label which guarantees its quality. Wines made in the south of Andalucia are sold under the Denominación de Origen "Montilla-Moriles". The finest extra-virgen oils made from olives grown on the high ground and mountains of southern Cordoba are classified as Aceite de Baena and Aceite de Priego.

Visiers' House, Medina Azahara (above) ▶
Medina Azahara (below)
Baena ▼

Down-river along the Guadalquivir is the castle of **Almodóvar del Río**. This splendid and well-preserved Gothic-Mudéjar fortress was built in the 14th century over Arab foundations. It was the favourite retreat of Pedro I, who kept his most valuable treasures and his prisoners in its dungeons. Turning up-river again, we reach **Montoro**, whose historic town centre of red stone and whitewash lies on a bend in the river.

Higher ground

To the south of Cordoba the land rises and the corn-fields give way to vineyards and olive groves. These hills shelter towns known for their art and their hospitality, as well as their wines and olive oil. **Baena** is one of the olive oil capitals, whose character and culture is to be discovered in the town's museums and olive presses. The layout of the old town offers a route around Arab walls, churches and monasteries such as Santa María and Madre de Díos, both 16th-century, as well as fine secular Baroque architecture and typical humbler buildings. **Montilla** is the centre of one the oldest wine-growing regions in Andalucía which produces the famous finos, amontillados and olorosos of Montilla-Moriles. Wineries stand side by side with historic

Church of the Assumption, Priego ▶
Gypsy pilgrimage, Cabra (above) ▼
Fuente del Rey, Priego (below)

buildings (the castle, church of Santiago and convent of Santa Clara) in this historic town, home of the noble family of Fernández de Córdoba. At the southern tip of the province in Lucena, a hard-working and entrepreneurial town known as the "The Pearl of Sephardy" in the Middle Ages as it housed one of the principal Jewish communities in Spain. Among the notable buildings are the Castle of Moral and the parish church of Saint Matthew (15th-16th centuries) with the astonishing Chapel of the Sacrarium dating from 1772, a masterpiece of the ornate Baroque style that flourished in the South of Cordoba in the 18th century.

Castles and fortresses

The land that was the frontier zone in the Middle Ages between the Christians and Muslims, as well as the estates of the great nobles saw the construction of numerous castles, fortified towns, turrets and watch towers. These can be seen throughout the south of Cordoba. Notable examples are the castles of Almodóvar, Montemayor, Espejo, Priego, Luque and Zuheros, and the walled towns of Baena, Montilla, Aguilar and Iznájar.

The Sierras Subbéticas

The slopes of the Sierras Subbéticas rise out of the countryside in a great mass of cliffs, gorges and hills in the last outcrop of the Mediterranean range. The ecological importance of this area has meant that its more than 30,000 hectares have been categorised as the Natural Park of the Sierras Subbéticas. It features towns dotted with towers such as Zuheros and Luque and cities such as Cabra and Priego, all exceptionally rich in architecture and art. The Archaeology Museum of **Cabra** covers its long history, also to be appreciated in the Plaza Vieja and the narrow streets of the Villa quarter, beneath the mound with the castle of the Counts of Cabra and the Church of the Assumption (16th-18th centuries), with its fine altarpieces and columns of red jasper from local quarries. Between groves of trees and orchards, **Priego de Córdoba** has the most famous Baroque centre, created in the 18th century in a town that was already important in the Middle Ages. The castle, the path behind the old walls, the narrow streets of the old quarter, all convey its Arabic past, while the church of the Assumption (16th-18th centuries) and its spectacular Chapel of the Sacrarium of 1772, as well as the church of the Aurora, all display the best of the Baroque; naves, domes and wall niches that became ornate, theatrical settings in which gesso decoration and paintings cover every available space. The most sophisticated interpretation of this virtuoso style is to be found in the pools and sculptures of **Fuente del Rey**, completed in the early 19th century.

Almodóvar del Río ▸

Jaén
Inland Paradise

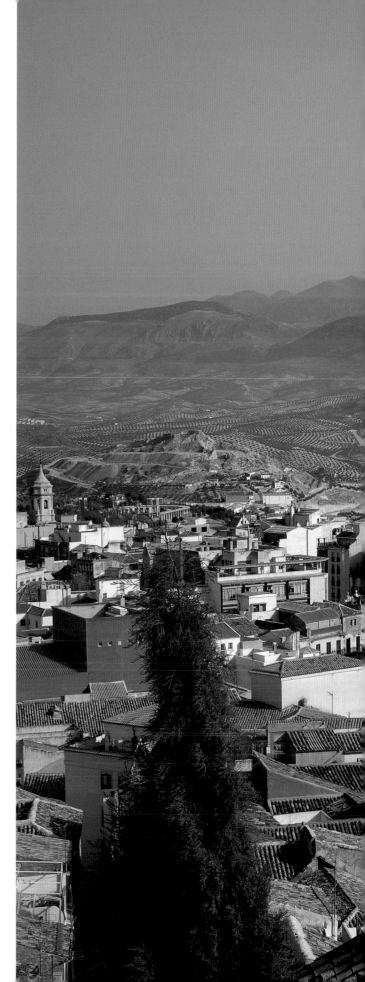

Jaén is the link between Andalucía and the Castilian plain or Meseta. The upper stretch of the Guadalquivir waters the vast "sea of olive trees" that characterises this province. It lies between the Sierra Morena in the north and the wild mountains to the south, and has the most impressive centres of art and architecture.

Jaén ▶

The Sierra Morena of Jaén

The castle, Jaén (below) ▶
Olivares (above) ▼
Jaén Cathedral (below)

Andújar, on the banks of the Guadalquivir and at the feet of the Sierra Morena, is one of the most important towns in Upper Andalucía. Its old centre focuses around the Plaza de España with the Town Hall (the former theatre built in the time of Philip IV) and the church of Saint Michael. The Church of Santa María (15th and 17th centuries) has major works of art such as the *Agony in the Garden* by El Greco. Along with the Clock Tower (16th century) it looks over the most typical part of the old town with its narrow streets. The Sierra Morena climbs up to the north of the city across the **Natural Park of the Sierra de Andújar**. In the heart of the mountains is the Sanctuary of the Virgin de la Cabeza, the destination for those taking part in Andalucía's most popular inland pilgrimage, which brings together half a million people in late April.

To the east of Andújar is the castle of **Baños de la Encina**, built by the Caliphs of Cordoba in the year 968 to guard the route into the interior from Castille, which today climbs up from Bailén to the pass at Despeñaperros, the gateway to Andalucía. To its south side is **La Carolina**, created in 1767 as the capital of the communities founded by Charles III to populate this region. Its carefully laid-out network of straight lines of streets is a textbook example of Enlightenment town planning. Down in the valley, **Linares** recalls the mining tradition in this province and the remains of the Iberian settlement of **Castulo**, whose sculptures and other splendid remains are on show in the local museum.

Jaén

Iberian and Roman in origin, **Jaén** became important as a "point along the trading route" (the meaning of its Arabic name, Yayyan) during the Muslim era, and as a fortified frontier town and the capital of the Christian kingdom following its reconquest by Ferdinand III in 1246. On the top of a rock is the **castle of Saint Catherine**, built by Arabs and Christians in the 12th and 13th centuries, offering an ideal viewing point over the city and the surrounding olive groves. The impressive bulk of the **Cathedral**, a masterpiece of Renaissance architecture, imposes itself over the surrounding old quarters that cling to the sides of the hill. The building was designed in the mid-16th century by Andrés de Vandelvira, whose work in the classical style is to be found throughout the city and its surroundings. The Chapter House and the Sacristy are the most obvious demonstrations of his talents. The façade, designed in 1668 by Eufrasio López de Rojas, consists of a two-storey design with giant order and corner towers, columns and a series of sculptures focusing on the figure of Saint

Ferdinand. Among the Cathedral's treasures is the relic of the Holy Face (Saint Veronica's Veil), as well as Flemish paintings, canvases by José de Ribera, goldsmiths' work and wrought iron work. The impressive Neo-classical **church of the Sacrarium** (late 18th century) by Ventura Rodríguez is attached to the end wall of the Cathedral. Nearby are the churches of Saint Ildefonso, and the Sanctuary of the Virgin de la Capilla, a building that covers all the main architectural styles between the 15th and 18th centuries.

The old quarter includes picturesque corners such as the calle Maestra, the Arch of San Lorenzo, the convent of Santa Clara and the Church of San Juan, extending to the parish church of Mary Magdalen (9th to 16th centuries), the heart of the medieval city. This still has its Islamic minaret and courtyard of the mosque, indicating its function prior to becoming a church. The square in front has a sculpture of the "Magdalen's lizard", illustrating the most famous local legend in which a young man killed the dragon that was terrorising the population, winning the annual tribute of a young maiden. In the basements of the nearby **Villardompardo Palace**, which now houses various museums, the "Baths of Ali" were discovered in 1913, comprising an extremely well preserved 11th-century Arab bath complex.

Jaén Cathedral ▶
Courtyard of the Hospital de Santiago, Úbeda ▼

The modern part of the city is the area around the **Plaza de la Constitución**, the Avenida de Madrid and the Paseo de la Estación, an area that also features the Battles Monument and the **Jaén Museum**. This has both archaeology and paintings sections, while the collection of Iberian art is the most important in Spain, with marvellous sculptures of warriors and animals dating from the 6th to 5th centuries BC.

Around Jaén

Above Jaén is the Sierra Sur, the imposing mountain range that borders Granada. At the entrance to the city is the fortified town of **La Guardia** and to the west **Martos**, a historic town with two castles and a famous mountain and whose name is synonymous with the cultivation of the olive, that fruitful tree whose name symbolises peace and civilisation. In Martos it becomes evident that the province of Jaén is the most important olive-oil producing region in the world, with more than 50 million trees and the highest production level in Spain. To the south of the mountains at around 60 kms from Jaén, is **Alcalá la Real**, a frontier town capped by the impressive fortress of La Mota and an abbatial church (16th-17th centuries).

Patrons and artists

The collaboration between a nobility that had grown rich as a result of the wars against the Muslims and the benefits reaped from Spain's colonial activities, and a large group of itinerant artists, resulted in the creation of magnificent Renaissance art in the cities of the region of Jaén in the 16th century. The most important patron was Francisco de Cobos (1480-1547), who funded the construction of churches, monasteries, palaces and castles in his native Úbeda, while the most important architect and sculptor was Andrés de Vandelvira (1505-1575), a native of La Mancha, who died in Jaén.

Palacio de las Cadenas, Úbeda ▲
Chapel of the Saviour, Úbeda ▶
Cathedral, Baeza page 114
Fountain of Santa María and Cathedral, Baeza page 115

Úbeda and Baeza

The banks of the upper Guadalquivir are home to the cities of Úbeda and Baeza. In 2003 they were both declared Patrimony of Humanity, reflecting the exceptional importance of these 16th-century cities. **Úbeda** lies on gentle slopes with its historic centre ringed by Arab walls. Few places can rival the Plaza Vázquez de Molina, the essence of Renaissance harmony. On one side is the Sacred Chapel of the Saviour, completed in 1556 with the contribution of Diego de Siloé and Andrés de Vandelvira as the pantheon of Francisco de los Cobos, Charles V's secretary and the figure who most encouraged the growth and splendour of his native town. The classicism of the Palacio de las Cadenas (Palace of the Chains), also by Vandelvira, forms another side of the square, opposite the church of Santa María de los Reales Alcázares, built from the 13th century onwards. Spreading out from here is a ring of cobbled streets and buildings with stone façades where time seems to have stood still, from the Plateresque Casa de las Tores (16th-century) to the church of Saint Paul (13th-16th centuries), the Casa Mudéjar (now a museum) and various impressive palaces, to the Plaza de Andalucía and the magnificent Hospital de Santiago built by Vandelvira between 1562 and 1575.

Plaza del Pópulo. Fountain of the Lions. Baeza (above) ▲
The Old University, Antonio Machado lecture hall, Baeza (below)
Palacio de Jabalquinto, Baeza ▶

On a nearby hill is **Baeza**, looking out onto the landscape praised by the poet Antonio Machado, who lived here for many years. A venerable city, when it passed into Christian hands in 1226 it was the centre for the conquest of Al-Andalus. The Cathedral includes Mudéjar and Gothic elements within the 16th-century Renaissance design by Vandelvira and Juan de Villalpando, who executed the façade in 1587. It presides over the Plaza de Santa María, a square of fine buildings with a graceful fountain designed as a triumphal arch. The surrounding streets reveal a number of fine buildings, such as the Jabalquinto Palace (15th-17th-centuries) which has one of the finest of all "flaming" Gothic façades, the church of the Holy Cross (13th century), a rare example of the Romanesque in Andalucía, and the old University of 1593. Below is the Castilian style square of the Mercado Viejo (Old Market), while the Plaza del Pópulo has the Casa del Pópulo, the old Meat Market, and the Villalar Arch around the Fountain of the Lions. Baeza has equally interesting outskirts, where we find the Town Hall, formerly the prison, with a highly sculptural, Plateresque façade, and numerous churches and fine houses.

The Sierras de Cazorla, Segura and Las Villas

The huge line of mountains formed by the Sierras of Cazorla, Segura and Las Villas enclose the province of Jaén to the east. This is a complex geometrical formation of abrupt cliffs, dense pinewoods and abundant water in which the Guadalquivir – *oued el-kebir*, the "great river" – begins its 657 km course. Beneath the Peña de los Halcones (Peak of the Falcons) is the attractive town of **Cazorla**, adapted to its sloping location between two castles, the Arab one known as the Castle of Five Corners, and the Christian one of La Yedra, open to visitors as a Museum and viewing point. On a higher slope is the romantic Templars' castle of La Iruela, which marks the pass to the largest area of protected land in Spain, the **Natural Park of the Sierras de Cazorla, Segura and Las Villas**, classified by Unesco as a Biospheric Reserve. With peaks of over 2,000 metres and areas of forest that could be elsewhere in the globe, this park covers an area of 214,000 hectares. Its landscapes are also the setting for outstandingly beautiful towns such as **Segura de la Sierra**, a romantic spot that typifies the charm of a medieval town, and **Hornos**, with its houses clinging to the edge of the ravine.

Olive oil from Jaén

Almost all the towns in this province, the most important oil-producing region in the world, produce extra-virgin oils. Of these, three have the Denominación de Origen label: the oil from the Sierra de Cazorla, from the Sierra de Segura and from the Sierra Mágina, three mountainous regions to the south of the province.

Segura de la Sierra (above) ▲
Mountain goat, Cazorla (below)
Tranco reservoir (above) ▶
Cazorla (below)

Granada
Gardens and snow

1. Alcazaba
2. Palace of Charles V, Alhambra and Fine Arts Museums
3. Nasrid Palaces
4. Church of Santa María de la Alhambra
5. Convent of San Francisco
6. Generlife
7. Bañuelo
8. Casa de Castril, Archaeological Museum
9. Casa del Chapiz
10. Church of the Salvador
11. Palace of Dar al-Horra, convent of Santa Isabel la Real
12. Cathedral
13. Royal Chapel
14. Hospital of San Juan de Dios
15. Monastery of San Jerónimo
16. Corral del Carbón
17. Casa de los Tiros
18. Torres Bermejas
19. Rodríguez-Acosta Foundation
20. House of Manuel de Falla
21. Carmen de los Mártires

Granada represents all the enchantment of Andalucía. The charms of the Alhambra and of a city which offers ever more delights the better one gets to know it, are repeated across the entire province, from the massive mountain range of the Sierra Nevada and the Alpujarras, to the eternal spring of the Costa Tropical.

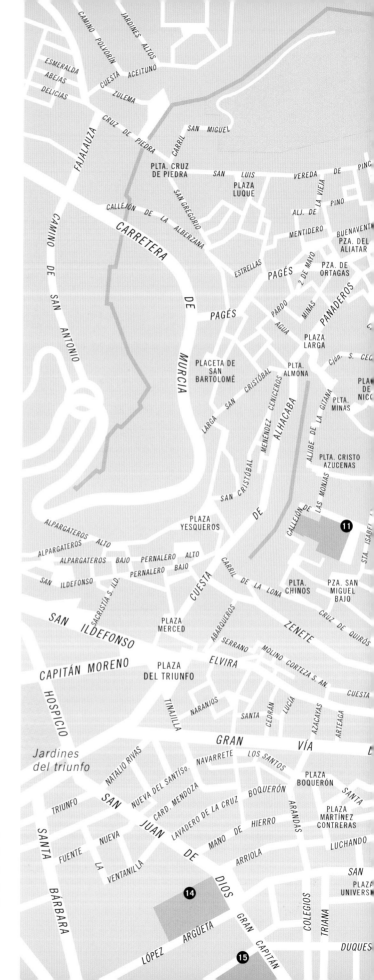

SACROMONTE

RÍO DARRO

0   150   300   450 m

Jardines del Generalife

PASEO   DE   LAS   ADELFAS

Aparcamento de la Alhambra

6

Huertas del Generalife

CAMINO FUENTE DEL AVELLANO

CUESTA   DE   LOS   CHINOS

CAMINO DEL SACROMONTE

9

CHAPIZ

CUESTA DEL REY CHICO

BOSQUE DE LA ALHAMBRA

5

AVDA. GENERALIFE

Jardines del Partal

ALHAMBRA

3

4

2

PLAZA DE LOS ALJIBES

8

ALBAYZÍN

BOSQUE   DE   LA   ALHAMBRA

21

PASEO DE LOS MÁRTIRES

ANTEQUERUELA ALTA

MATAMOROS

Cjón.

20

ANTEQUERUELA   BAJA

7
Bañuelo

1

ROYO

NIÑO   DEL

CAMINO DEL REALEJO

PARRA DE S. CECILIO

CARRIL   DE SAN CECILIO

HOTELES DE BELÉN

PLAZA CRUZ VERDE

PLEGADERO   ALTO

PLEGADERO   BAJO

HUERTO S. CECILIO

NEVOT

BELÉN

CAMPO DEL PRÍNCIPE

19

CALLEJÓN

AIRE   ALTA

VERGELES

CUESTA   DEL   REALEJO

MOLINOS

CUARTELILLO

PLAZA SANTA ANA

ALTA   BAJA

ALMANZORA

ALMAN ZORA

18

CRUZ DE PIEDRA

ALAMILLOS

PTA.   DEL   SOL

STA.   CATALINA

DAMASQUEROS

PLAZA DEL REALEJO

JARRERÍA

SOMOSIERRA   GUADARRAMA

SANTIAGO

AVE. MARÍA

SOLARES

CUESTA   DE   GOMÉREZ

CUESTA   DE   MARAÑAS

Cta. PERRO

CÁRCEL ALTA

PLAZA NUEVA

CUESTA   NUEVA

CUESTA   RODRIGO   DEL   CAMPO

17

STA.   ESCOLÁSTICA

SECO   DE   LUCENA

MORAL

ALTA

CALLEJÓN DEL SEÑOR

SALVADOR

SOLARES

REYES

PAVANERAS

PLAZA SANTO DOMINGO

COLÓN

CALDERERÍA NUEVA

CALDERERÍA VIEJA

COLCHA

BALLESTEROS

JESÚS Y MARÍA

CAPITANÍA

PLAZA SAN JUAN DE LA CRUZ

PLAZA DESCALZAS

PLAZA ISABEL LA CATÓLICA

PALACIOS

CRUELLAS

PLACETA DE LOS CAMPOS

Cjón. DEL TINTE

CETTI-MERIEM

COSTA

ABENAMAR

SAN RAFAEL

VARELA

PROGRESO

CUESTA

ENRIQUETA LOZANO

CONCEPCIÓN

NICUESA

ANCHA DE LA VIRGEN

CASTAÑEDA

SAN JACINTO

MAESTRO ALONSO

13

16

CARMEN

TORILLO

JAZMÍN

A. CASTRO

HORNO

SAN MATÍAS

NARANJO

SANTA

SAN MATÍAS

LAS NAVAS

SARABIA

CERVANTES

PLAZA MARIANA PINEDA

MIRASOL

SAN PEDRO

MÁRTIR

PASEO   DEL   SALÓN

JERÓNIMO

DIEGO

SILOS

OFICIO

ESTRIBO

12

CÁRCEL

ALCAICERÍA

ZACATÍN

MARIANA PINEDA

LEPANTO

PLAZA DEL CARMEN

PIEDRA

ESCUDO

GOZO

ÁNGEL

GANIVET

PLAZA DEL CAMPILLO

RÍO GENIL

PASEO   DE   LOS

PLAZA PASIEGAS

PLAZA ROMANILLA

BOABDIL

CATÓLICOS

SALAMANCA

PLAZA DEL CAMPILLO

CARRERA   DEL   GENIL

PLAZA BIBARRAMBLA

PESCADERÍA

MESONES

PUERTA REAL

ACERA   DEL   CASINO

ACERA   DEL   DARRO

PLAZA TRINIDAD

TRINIDAD

LUCENA

HORNO DE MARINA

Granada

El Partal, Alhambra ▶
Courtyard of the Myrtles, Alhambra (above) ▼
Courtyard of the Lions, Alhambra (below)

The capital of Eastern Andalucía, Granada occupies a majestic location at the foot of the Sierra Nevada before the river valley of Genil. It was originally an Ibero-Roman town and the city of Elvira, until Garnata came into being in the 11th century as the capital of one of the Divided Kingdoms. Its finest period, however, was between the 13th and 15th centuries when it became the capital of the last Muslim kingdom of the Peninsula under Nasrid rule. When the Catholic Kings conquered it in 1492, it was one of the richest and largest cities in Europe. The monarchs further embellished it with large buildings, at the same time subjugating the Moriscos, the descendants of the Muslims. Granada acquired a unique character, the result of this symbiosis of civilisations, until it become one of the most admired cities in the world, an obligatory stopping-off point for travellers and a fertile source of artists and writers including as Federico García Lorca.

La Alhambra

The **Alhambra** is undoubtedly the highlight of Granada, as well as the most famous and visited monument in Andalucía and one of the wonders of world art, classified by UNESCO as Patrimony of Humanity. Its name means "the red" or *al-hamra* in Arabic, due to the colour of the walls around the outside of this large fortified city which was the home to the Nasrid court. The founder of this dynasty, the Emir Ibn Alhamar, began its construction in 1238, subsequently enlarged by his successors Yusuf I and Muhammad V in the 14th century. A wood with water courses running through it surrounds the whole complex, reached via entrances such as the Justice Doorway (1348). The keystone of the arches have the sign of the open hand, a talisman of good luck, and the key, the Nasrid emblem. The Plaza de los Aljibes, in front of the Wine Doorway, leads into the different areas of the Alhambra. Particularly striking is the contrast with the **Palace of Charles V**, a Renaissance building designed in 1527 by Pedro Machuca on a square ground-plan with a circular courtyard, now housing the Alhambra and Fine Arts Museums.

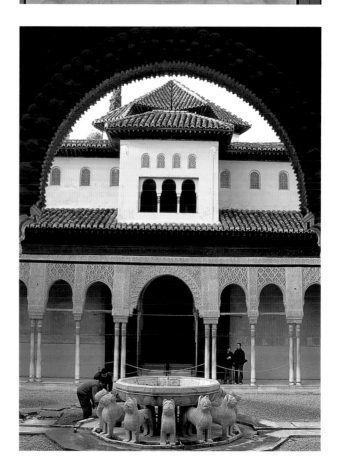

The front part of the complex has the palace-fortress of the **Alcazaba**, the oldest part of the Alhambra, with the massive Candle Tower which dominates the city. Next to the Palace of Charles V is the visitor entrance into the very heart of the Alhambra, the so-called **Nasrid Palaces**, a group of royal apartments of remarkable refinement. Using delicate materials – brick, gesso, tiles and wood – and a sophisticated use of water and plants, this by now declining kingdom created an earthly paradise of a moving beauty and

sensuality in which art and nature blend in vibrant equilibrium. The first group of rooms is the **Mexuar**, with the Golden Chamber and the gesso façade dating from 1369. Next is the Comares Palace, the focus of official life, with the pool of the Patio de los Arrayanes (Courtyard of the Myrtles) which reflects the Comares Tower. Inside is the Hall of the Ambassadors, or the Throne Room, beneath a wooden dome representing the heavens. The rich decoration of tiles, arabesque and inscriptions covers the walls and passageways that lead to the **Courtyard of the Lions**, the private house of the sultan (1343-1377). Its forest of fine columns and the Hall of the Monarchs, of the Two Brothers and of the Abencerrajes are sublimely beautiful. Corridors connect to the Royal Baths, the Viewing Terrace of Lindaraja and various rooms and courtyards leading to the Partal Gardens and the Ladies' Tower. The walls support towers that house the palatial rooms of the Cautiva (1340) and the Infantas (15th century). On the Hill of the Sun, above the Alhambra, is the **Generalife**, the recreational estate of the royal family with its splendid gardens and a pavilion (15th century), with the jets of the Water Channel Courtyard in front.

The Alhambra from the San Nicolás viewing-point (page 124)
Courtyard of the Palace of Charles V ▶
Paseo de los Tristes ▼

The River Darro and the Albayzín

The River Darro runs between the Alhambra and the Albayzín. It flows beneath the **Plaza Nueva**, flanked by the Royal Chancelllery and the Mudéjar church of Santa Ana (16th century), and by the lively atmosphere of the inns and bars that line the nearby streets. Up-river is the romantic **Carrera del Darro**, that leads to the Bañuelo, the 11th-century Arab baths, and the **Casa de Castril** (now the Archaeology Museum). Sloping up from the Darro are the lanes of the quarter known as the **Albayzín**, the main Morisco quarter of the city. A walk around its twisting and turning streets transports the visitor back to another age, wandering past the fine houses with gardens known as **cármenes** (private residences with tiered gardens of box hedges and cypress trees), Arab houses like those in the calle Chapiz, churches built over mosques like the church of El Salvador, and convents such as Santa Isabel la Real which includes the Palace of Dar al-Horra, and the house of the Sultaness Aixa, mother of the last king of Granada, the unfortunate Boabdil. Finally we reach the **viewing-point of San Nicolás**, the most famous in the city, opposite the Alhambra and looking across to the Sierra Nevada. Behind the Albayzín is the gypsy quarter of the **Sacromonte** with its famous caves.

Federico García Lorca

Granada and various villages in its river valley are closely linked to the life of this Andalucian poet and playwright, possibly Spain's most internationally-famed literary figure. Born in 1898 in the country town of Fuente Vaqueros, Lorca spent his summers at the Huerta de San Vicente just outside Granada. In August 1936 he was killed in the nearby village of Víznar by Franco's rebels.

View of tha Albayzín from the Alhambra ▶
Sacromonte (left) ▼
Chancellery (right)

The centre and the lower city

On the plain at the feet of the Alhambra and the Albayzín is the historical city centre, in which the Christian and more recent aspects of Granada are more evident. The **Gran Vía**, the Plaza de Isabel la Católica and the calle Reyes Católicos to the Puerta Real (Royal Gateway) are the main streets in the city centre. The **Cathedral** is the most important monument. Begun in 1523 by Enrique Egas in the Gothic style, it was transformed by Diego de Siloé into a masterpiece of Renaissance architecture, completed in the 17th century by the façade, designed by Alonso Cano. Particularly notable is the **Main Chapel**, an outstanding piece of architectural measuring 45 metres high, as well as the oil paintings and sculptures by the Granadan artist Alonso Cano. Next to the Cathedral is the **Royal Chapel**, built in the Florid Gothic style and completed by Enrique Egas in 1521. It houses the tombs of the Catholic Kings, as well as Philip The Fair and Juana La Loca. The Carrara marble tombs, the wrought-iron grilles and the collections of paintings assembled by Queen Isabel, with works by Memling, Botticelli and Perugino, among others, all make this chapel and its contents outstanding. Nearby is the **Madraza** or Old Counsel House, with a 14th-century Islamic oratory, the former Arab market of the Alcaicería (rebuilt) the shopping street of Zacatín, the **Corral del Carbon** (14th-century), the grain market where goods and merchants met, and the Plaza Bibarrambla, an agreeable spot lined with cafes and florists. Towards the west are various barrios extending to the University, the hospital and the magnificent Baroque church of San Juan de Dios (18th-century), and the monastery of Saint Jerome, founded by the Gran Capitán in 1496, with a Renaissance cloister and church of astonishing decorative richness. By now we have reached the Campo del Triunfo and the Royal Hospital (16th century).

From the Puerta Real to the Genil runs an old quarter with bustling areas such as the **Campo del Príncipe**, below the Mauror or Jewish quarter and the area known as Antequeruela. Numerous places of interest are to be found here, such as the house that was the birthplace of the musician Manuel da Falla, the *carmenes* of the Martyrs and of the Fundación Rodríguez Acosta and the Renaissance Casa de los Tiros.

Around Granada

There are a wealth of attractive places to visit on the outskirts of the town and in the river valley. These include the **Carthusian Monastery** on the outskirts of Granada, whose plain exterior does not prepare the visitor for the brilliant exuberance of its Sacristy, dating from 1764, and the

Corral del Carbón (above) ▲
Bibarrambla square (below)
Granada Cathedral (above) ▶
The Royal Chapel (below)

Sancta Sanctorum, both masterpieces of Spanish Baroque. García Lorca is commemorated in the museums of the **Huerta de San Vicente**, where the poet spent his summers, and in the house where he was born at **Fuente Vaqueros** in the valley. Also lying on this area of cultivated land is Santa Fe, a historic place where the Catholic Kings prepared the assault on Granada and agreed with Christopher Columbus the terms of his voyage. Located in the mountains about 50 kms to the west of the capital is a curve of historic towns whose appearance records their role as frontier bastions: Montefrío, Loja, Alhama de Granada, the latter set against a vertiginous gorge and also known for a famous spa.

Guadix and the Cenete

The entire province of Granada still has many little known and surprising areas. This is the case with the north of the region, a landscape of plains with marvellous colours, of valleys and gardens sheltered by the Sierra Nevada. Here we find **Guadix** (45 kms from Granada), with a splendid Baroque Cathedral (18th century), and winding quarters of cave-houses. A short distance away is **Baza** with its rival Cathedral (16th century). Tucked in the folds of the hills are the towns of the **Marquisate of Cenete**,

Guadix (above) ▲
The alcazaba, Guadix (below)
La Calahorra ▶

watched over by the castle-palace of **La Calahorra**, one of the early examples of Renaissance architecture in Spain, built by Italian workmen in 1512 on the order of a legendary marquis who ultimately never lived there.

The Sierra Nevada

Following the course of the Genil from Granada, a road climbs up the highest mountains in Spain, the **Sierra Nevada**, the peaks of perpetual snows with the most southerly ski resort in Europe. The Pradollano complex, 35 kms from the capital and 2,100 metres high, has an excellent range of hotels and sporting facilities. This Alpine-type range, of huge ecological and aesthetic importance, unique in Andalucía, was declared a **National Park** in 1999. It covers 86,000 hectares. The flora and fauna of the highest peaks, the glacial lakes and the line of peaks of more than 3,000 metres make the Sierra Nevada the ideal place for those looking to find nature in its purest state. The highest peaks are those of the Veleta and the **Mulhacén** (3,482) metres, the latter named after one of the last Sultans of Granada, Muley al-Hasan, whose desire it was to be buried on its frozen peak.

The Alpujarras and the Tropical Coast

To the south of Granada lie the gates to paradise. Or at least the part of Andalucía that comes closest to it, the Alpujarras, on the south slopes of the Sierra Nevada. The uniqueness of this region is mainly due to the its position on huge spurs of rock, making it a century-old bastion of traditions, with an outstanding landscape of cultivated terraces, forests, roaring torrents and white villages with flat clay roofs. It is not surprising that this was the last refuge of the Moors in their final battles, and that they left behind the marks of their presence which have lasted over the centuries. Today their footsteps are retraced by visitors in search of peace and harmony between man and the natural habitat. **Lanjarón**, a village of spas and crystalline waters, is the gateway to this region, while **Órgiva**, in the Guadalfeo valley, is the capital of the western part. Above, in the clouds, is the **Upper Alpujarras**, with a spectacular route running from the **Poqueira Gorge**, which houses Pampaneira, Bubión and Capileira, continuing towards Pitres and its villages towards Trevélez, the highest village in Spain at 1,600 metres. Its dry air makes it ideal for the production of hams and cured pork. The Alpujarras continue for many kilometres more towards Cádiar and Ugíjar, finally ending in the province of Almería at Laujar de Andarax.

To the South of Granada
The impressive landscapes and remote feel of the villages in the Alpujarras have attracted visitors from all over the world since the middle of the last century, in particular artists and creative figures. The result is a veritable foreign colony of the most cosmopolitan sort. One of the pioneers was the Hispanophile Englishman Gerald Brenan (1894-1987), who made this area world famous with his book *To the South of Granada*, in which he recounts numerous incidents in his life as well as local customs and events.

Capileira (above) ▲
Sierra Nevada (below) ▶
Poqueira ravine, Bubión and Capileira (below)

The snowy mountains of the Alpjurras fall swiftly down over around 40kms to the plantations of sugar cane and exotic crops of the **Costa Tropical** (Tropical Coast) of Granada, on the shores of the Mediterranean, creating an astonishing contrast. To the west is **Almuñécar**, founded by the Phoenicians with the name of Sexi, focused around the castle of San Miguel and surrounded by bays, cliffs and fascinating beaches, such as the Herradura (Horseshoe Beach). **Salobreña** is a cluster of whitewashed houses with an Arabic feel on a promontory capped by an Arabic fortress, a splendid balcony over the sea, the river valley of the Guadalfeo and the surrounding mountains. **Motril** is the largest city, with a tradition of sugar-cane production which dates back to the Nasrid period (in past times it was known as "Little Cuba"). It looks on to the Mediterranean with its commercial and fishing port, and its crowded holiday resorts such as Torrenueva. To the east, the Tropical Coast continues via Castell de Ferro and a line of watch-towers, castles and villages at the feet of the Sierra de la Contraviesa, extending to the province of Almería.

Salobreña ▶
Almuñécar ▼

Almería
Eastern Andalucía

Almería is Andalucía's most Mediterranean and eastern province, with a dramatic mountain interior, cultivated river valleys and deserts, and a fascinating coastline of beaches and bays of transparent water.

Tabernas desert ▶

Almería

On the shores of the Mediterranean lies Almería meaning "mirror of the sea", the name given to it by the Arabs when they founded it over 1,000 years ago. The city exudes an exotic and tranquil air with its commercial and fishing port, squares and avenues planted with palm trees and its luminous façades at the foot of the Sierra de Gádor.

The **Alcazaba** (palace-fortress) is the largest in the Peninsula, dominating Almería from a rocky hillside. Built between the 10th and 15th centuries, its three different areas enclose towers and bastions as well as the remains of palaces which were inhabited by an independent court in the 11th century. From the Fortress we look over the humble barrios of cave-houses which spread over the slopes of the hill, down towards the **Plaza Vieja** (Old Square), also known as the Plaza de la Constitución, now the Town Hall and the main focus of the old city centre. Close by is the **Cathedral**, a massive bulwark of stone begun in 1524, at a time when the threat of pirates and Moors marked the rhythm of life in the city. The Cathedral fuses Gothic elements (the main chapel and vaults) and Renaissance ones (the entrances and the chapel of the Pietà), and houses numerous works of art such as paintings by Alonso Cano, the 16th-century choirstalls and the great marble and jasper tabernacle. On one of the façades we see the Portocarrero Sun, a relief of a sun with a human face, symbol of the city.

Down towards the port run the oldest streets of the Muslim quarter, the church of San Juan (built in the 17th century over a mosque) which lead towards the **Nicolás Salmerón Park**, with its view of the ferries that run between the city and North Africa. In the distance, on the waterfront is the iron structure of the so-called "English Cable", a jetty constructed in 1904 as the outlet for the mines which were dotted all over the surrounding mountains between the mid-19th and mid-20th centuries.

The lively, colourful nature of Almería is particularly evident in the Paseo de Almería and the **Puerta de Purchena**, the heart of town, filled with shops, terraces and examples of Art Nouveau Architecture. Close by is the bustle of the Central Market, with its exhibition of seafood and locally grown fruit and vegetables, as well as more peaceful spots, such as the Renaissance church of Santiago (16th century), the Plaza de las Flores (Square of the Flowers) and the Plaza de San Pedro, the monastery of Santo Domingo (18th century, now a cultural centre), and the Sanctuary of the Virgin of the Sea, the patron saint of the city. The broad avenue called the **Rambla de Belén** separates the old town from the city from the more modern part of the city which spreads into the valley and along the beaches of Almería to Gabo de Gata.

The alcazaba, Almería (above) ▲
Sierra de Gádor (below)
Plaza Vieja (Plaza de la Constitución), Almería ▶

Around Almería

To the west of the capital is the region known as **Poniente**, with its "sea of plastic" created by the covered cultivation of vegetables that has made Almería into one of the leading producers in Europe and which spreads down towards the coast. This coastline of long beaches is characterised by residential complexes, yachting harbours, golf courses and other facilities, extending from the tourist resorts of **Aguadulce** and **Roquetas de Mar**, to the Almerimar complex in El Ejido, and the historic city of **Adra**, "The first soil that the Phoenicians stepped on when they arrived in Iberia".

The Tabernas desert

Behind Almería are the hills and dry riverbeds of the **Tabernas Desert**, the only desert region in continental Europe. The village of Tabernas lies on the flat at the foot of a hill with the remains of an Arab fortress. The stunning beauty of its surroundings has made it the setting for numerous films, mainly "spaghetti-westerns", along with famous ones such as *Cleopatra* and *Indiana Jones*. To film *Death had its Price* a Wild West town was built in the

The Indalo

This unusual symbol which represents the province of Almería is a schematic human figure whose arms are extended into a semicircle that closes above its head, suggesting the sun. It was created by the painter Jesús de Perceval, who was inspired by a number of pre-historic paintings found in Vélez Blanco and by the simple motifs painted on the village houses in Mojácar as magic talismans to ward off the evil eye.

Adra (above) ▶
Roquetas de Mar (below)
Tabernas desert ▼

desert, one of a number in so-called *Mini-Hollywood* where stunt men perform action scenes to surprised tourists.

The Cabo de Gata and Níjar

The charm of Almería continues inland in the mountains and along the coastline of the Cabo de Gata, undoubtedly one of the most unique and striking regions of Andalucía. The dry expanses of volcanic rock outline a shoreline of cliffs, reefs, bays and beaches of crystal clear water, a natural paradise. These majestic landscapes, bearing almost no signs of human habitation, make up the **Natural Terrestial-Maritime** park covering 26,000 underwater hectares, striking rock formations and sand dunes, the latter the chosen venue for some scenes in the Oscar-winning *Lawrence of Arabia*. From the visitor centre in Amoladeras, the damp ground of Las Salinas and the promontory with its lighthouse at Cabo de Gata, the coast continues to the east with magic places such as Monsul and Los Genoveses, dotted with a line of watchtowers, castles and old fishing villages such as San José, Los Escullos, Las

Coastline of the Cabo de Gata ▶
Lighthouse of the Cabo de Gata ▼

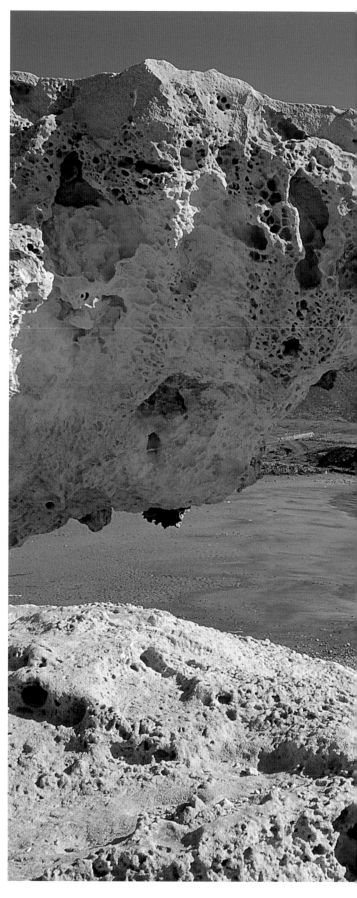

Negras and Agua Amarga, from which the sun can be seen rising over the Mediterranean.

Moving inland, in the brown-grey heart of the Sierra Alhamilla is **Níjar**, a particularly beautiful town of white-washed Moorish-style houses lying between orchards and cultivated terraces. Its geometrical profile, created by the typical architecture of this region, with its clean cubic shapes, is arranged around a fortified church in the Mudéjar style (16th century). Níjar's traditional roots are also to be found in its local ceramics characterised by metallic glazes, and its brightly-coloured cotton rugs made from scraps of cloth.

Mojácar, Eastern Almería and Los Vélez

The eastern end of Almería or the **Levante** is also the most easterly end of Andalucía. Here the coastline becomes less rugged and opens up into large beaches. **Mojácar** rises up like a sweep of white against the hillside, clustered into a picturesque labyrinth of steep slopes and narrow streets. The viewing terraces in the upper town offer splendid panoramic views, while the little Square of the Flowers and other spots share the relaxed atmosphere of the town, now a popular tourist venue. Below the town lies

Mojácar (above) ▲
The fishing port of Garrucha (below)
San José ▶

Mojácar Beach and the shoreline that runs to **Garrucha**, the main port of Eastern Almería. Between Garrucha and the boundary with Murcia is **Vera**, set in a cultivated river valley running down to marvellous beaches, and **Cuevas de Almanzora**, a town that saw its finest hour in the 19th century thanks to the mining industry. It has a notable castle (16th century) and the caves excavated in the hillsides. The Almerian Levante comes to an end in front of the islet of **San Juan de los Terreros**.

Inland is the region of Los Vélez, in the north of Almería. Its wooded mountains with pines and holm oaks contrast with the landscape of the rest of this region and are now categorised as the **Natural Park of the Sierra de María**, an oasis of green between limestone peaks. The main town are **Vélez Rubio**, with its Baroque church of the Incarnation (18th century) and **Vélez Blanco**, a medieval town topped by a Renaissance castle built by the Marqués de los Vélez in the early 16th century, and one of the most impressive fortresses in the whole of Andalucía.

Vélez Blanco ▶
Mojácar ▼

Leisure

● Public holidays

Not for nothing is Andalucía considered the most fun-loving, outgoing and festive region of Spain, with one of the most packed and varied calendars of public holidays, particularly in spring and summer. Flamenco dancing and bullfighting usually take place at the larger fairs and on the main holidays.

The Procession of the Three Kings. 5 January. Lively procession with floats in the centre of the provincial capitals and main cities.

Carnival. Starts in February, dates variable. Particularly important and colourful in Cadiz, where it is the main annual festival. Crowds in fancy dress and masks invade the streets in cheerful chaos, between processions of floats and competitions among the various singing groups.

Andalucía Day. 28 February, annual festival of the Region of Andalucía.

Easter Week. March-April. Dates vary. Easter Week celebrations mark the arrival of spring. They involve spectacular processions of splendid religious images on elaborate bases, accompanied by groups of Nazarenes and penitents. They are all worth seeing, from the smallest villages to the large cities, but the most famous are those held in Seville and Malaga, each with its own style,

▼ *The Seville Fair*

as well as those in Cadiz, Cordoba and Granada.

Fairs. April-October. Dates varying according to place. Fairs and fiestas, whose origins lie in the old livestock fairs or patron saint days, are held in many villages in Andalucía in areas especially intended for such celebrations and laid out with little booths, walkways and attractions. On display are horsemen and women and horse-drawn carriages, while many of those taking part dress up in regional dress and enjoy the singing and dancing that forms the heart of such events. The April Fair in Seville is the first of these, followed by the Horse Fair in Jerez in early May and the Feria de la Salud in Cordoba at the end of that month. The Fiestas Colombinas in Huelva take place in early August, while the Malaga Fair is half-way through the month and the Almería Fair at the end. The Feria de San Lucas in Jaén is the last, around 18 October.

Romerías. April-October. Dates vary. Romerías or pilgrimage-celebrations to rural shrines are profoundly Andalucian celebrations that keep alive the rural traditions of the region. Pilgrims, on foot and on horseback or travelling in decorated carts and other forms of transport make their way, sometimes taking days, to the chosen shrine, resulting in an extended celebration held in the middle of the countryside. From spring to the beginning of autumn this takes place throughout the region. The most famous are those of the Virgin del Rocío in Almonte (Huelva) in late May or early June and the Virgen de la Cabeza in Andújar (Jaén), in late April.

May Crosses. Around 3 May. Interior courtyards and squares in the old quarters are decorated with crosses, altars, flowers and hangings and become meeting-places for celebrations. These take place throughout the region, but those in Cordoba are the most splendid and famous.

Corpus Christi. End of May/early June. The streets are decorated with flowers and hangings for the solemn Corpus Christi processions, particularly notable in the provincial capitals and county towns as well as in the Sierra de Cadiz and in numerous villages. In Granada, this festival is also the main fiesta of the city, with processions of giants and figures with huge carnival heads as well as several days of fun.

Feast of San Juan (Saint John). 24 June. On the night before the Saint's day, bonfires are lit in village streets.

Virgen del Carmen (The Carmelite Virgin). 16 July. A popular and widespread festival, particularly important on the coast where small boats take part in marine processions.

Moors and Christians. Summer. Dates vary. An unusual festival involving opposing bands dressed in medieval costume. Found in numerous mountain villages in eastern Andalucía.

The Assumption of the Virgin. 15 August. Religious festival with numerous processions of the various virgins associated with local devotional cults.

Harvest Festival. September. Dates vary. Particularly important in grape-producing areas such as Jerez and its surrounding villages.

Flamenco and the Bullfight

The real origins of Spain's folkloric culture lie in Andalucía, source of inspirations for numerous internationally-renowned performers such as Paco de Lucía. Flamenco has its home in the popular quarters of Jerez, Seville, Cadiz and Cordoba, and in the cities and villages of the region. The region's fairs and festivals are brought to life with flamenco singing and the dancing of sevillanas, while the art of "cante hondo", of guitar playing and singing is to be enjoyed in the numerous summer Flamenco festivals, in amateur clubs, night-clubs and theatres, as well as in events such as the Seville Flamenco

Biennial. The latter brings together in September the greatest figures in the field. With regard to the bullfight, Andalucía is home to some of the most famous of all fighters such as Joselito, Belmonte, Manolete and Curro Romero, while it also houses some of the most celebrated rings such as those in Puerto de Santa María, Cordoba and Malaga. The spirit of the bullfight is nowhere better expressed than in the unique atmosphere of the April Fair in Seville, the summer bullfights held in Puerto de Santa María and the bullfights held in Ronda in September in which those taking part dress in the costume of Goya's era.

The Immaculate Conception.
8 December. Festival, in some places celebrated the night before.
Verdiales. 28 December. Ancient festival of the Malaga region, with "pandas" or groups of musicians who sing, accompanied by guitars and violins.

Museums

Almería
Museo de Almería
Prehistoric Room.
Biblioteca Pública Francisco Villaespesa.
C/ Hermanos Machado s/n.
Tel. 950 264 492

Cadiz
Museo de Cadiz
Plaza de Mina s/n.
Tel. 956 212 281
Museo Catedralicio
Plaza de Fray Félix s/n.
Tel. 956 259 812
Museo de las Cortes y Sitio de Cádiz
C/ Santa Inés, 9.
Tel. 956 221 788

Córdoba
Museo Arqueológico y Etnológico
Plaza de Jerónimo Páez, 7.
Tel. 957 474 011
Museo de Bellas Artes y Museo Julio Romero de Torres
Plaza del Potro, 1.
Tel. 957 473 345 / 957 491 909

Easter Week ▼

Museo Diocesano de Bellas Artes
C/ Torrijos, 12.
Tel. 957 479 375
Museo Municipal Taurino
Plaza de Maimónides, 1.
Tel. 957 201 056
Museo Vivo de al-Andalus
Puente Romano, Torre de la Calahorra
Tel. 957 293 929

Granada
Casa Museo Federico García Lorca
Huerta de San Vicente.
C/ Virgen Blanca s/n.
Tel. 958 258 466
http://huertadesanvicente.com
Casa Museo Manuel de Falla
C/ Antequeruela Alta, 11.
Tel. 958 222 188
Museo de la Alhambra y de Bellas Artes
Alhambra, Palacio de Carlos V.
Tel. 958 220 912 /
958 224 843
Museo Arqueológico y Etnológico
Carrera del Darro, 41.
Tel. 958 225 640
Museo Casa de los Tiros
C/ Pavaneras, 19.
Tel. 958 220 629
Museo de la Catedral
C/ Gran Vía, 4.
Tel. 958 222 959

Huelva
Museo de Huelva
Alameda Sundheim, 13.
Tel. 959 259 300

Jaén
Museo de Artes y Costumbres Populares, Baños Árabes
Palacio de Villardompardo.
Plaza Santa Luisa de Marillac s/n.
Tel. 953 236 292
Museo Catedralicio
Catedral. Plaza de Santa María s/n.
Tel. 953 234 233
Museo de Jaén
Paseo de la Estación, 27.
Tel. 953 274 507

Málaga
Museo de Artes y Costumbres Populares
Pasillo de Santa Isabel, 10.
Tel. 952 217 137
Museo Casa Natal Pablo Ruiz Picasso
Plaza de la Merced, 32.
Tel. 952 060 215
http://fundacionpicasso.es

The Fine Arts Museum, Seville ▲

Museo Catedralicio
Catedral. C/ Molina Larios s/n.
Tel. 952 215 917
Museo Picasso
Palacio de Buenavista
C/ San Agustín, 8.
Tel. 902 443 377
http://museopicassomalaga.org
Museo Taurino
Plaza de toros de la Malagueta.
Paseo de Reding, 16.
Tel. 952 226 292

Seville
Centro Andaluz de Arte Contemporáneo
Monasterio de la Cartuja.
Isla de la Cartuja s/n.
Tel. 955 037 083
Museo Arqueológico
Plaza de América s/n.
Tel. 954 232 401
Museo de Artes y Costumbres Populares
Plaza de América, 3.
Tel. 954 232 576
Museo de Bellas Artes
Plaza del Museo, 9.
Tel. 954 220 790
Museo Catedralicio
Catedral. Plaza Virgen de los Reyes s/n.
Tel. 954 214 971
Museo Marítimo
Torre del Oro.
Paseo de Cristóbal Colón s/n.
Tel. 954 222 419
Museo Taurino de la Plaza de Toros
Paseo de Cristóbal Colón, 12.
Tel. 954 210 315
http://realmaestranza.com

A flamenco performance ▲

The performing arts

A selection of the main venues for theatre, concerts, dance and opera in the region's provincial capitals

Almería
Auditorio Municipal Maestro Padilla
Avenida del Mediterráneo s/n.
Tel. 950 273 411
Cádiz
Gran Teatro Falla
Plaza de Falla s/n.
Tel. 956 220 834
Córdoba
Gran Teatro
C/ Gran Capitán, 3.
Tel. 957 480 644
Granada
Auditorio Manuel de Falla
Paseo de los Mártires s/n.
Tel. 958 222 188
Huelva
Gran Teatro
C/ Vázquez López, 13.
Tel. 959 245 703
Jaén
Teatro Darymelia
C/ Colón s/n.
Tel. 953 219 116
Malaga
Teatro Cervantes
C/ Ramos Marín s/n.
Tel. 952 224 100
Seville
Teatro de la Maestranza
Paseo de Colón, 22.
Tel. 954 223 344

Golf and skiing

Golf. Andalucía offers frankly magnificent opportunities for playing golf and enjoys world-wide fame among enthusiasts of this sport as a consequence. Both the number, quality and design of the courses as well as the length of the season which extends throughout the year make it a renowned golfing centre. Currently the region has dozens of golf courses spread over every province, but mainly along the coast: 38 in Malaga, 16 in Cadiz, 8 in Huelva, 7 in Almería, 4 in Seville, 2 in Cordoba, 2 in Granada and 1 in Jaén.
Federación Andaluza de Golf (Andalucían Golf Federation)
C/ Sierra de Grazalema, 35, 5. Málaga.
Tel. 952 225 590
http://golf-andalucia.net
Skiing. The Pradollano ski station is located in the Sierra Nevada near Granada. This is the most southerly ski station in Europe and offers an unusual leisure option in Spain's sunniest region.
Cetursa-Sierra Nevada
Plaza de Andalucía Sierra Nevada
(Granada)
Tel. 902 708 090
http://sierranevadaski.com

Andalucía with Children

Almería
Mini Hollywood
A Wild West town in the middle of the desert: actually a film set with action scenes played out by stunt men for visitors.

Carretera Nacional 340, km 4,6. Tabernas.
Tel. 950 365 236
Cádiz
Zoo Botánico Jerez
A carefully-looked after and very comprehensive collection of animals and plant life
C/ Taxdirt s/n. Jerez de la Frontera.
Tel. 956 182 397
http://zoobotanicojerez.com
Granada
Parque de las Ciencias
Large modern venue with planetarium and interactive attractions.
Avenida del Mediterráneo s/n.
Tel. 958 131 900
http://parqueciencias.com
Huelva
Parque Nacional de Doñana
Organised visits to the National Doñana Park.
El Rocío, Almonte.
Avenida de la Canaliega s/n.
Tel. 959 443 808
http://turismodedonana.com
Málaga
Parque de Atracciones Tívoli World
Arroyo de la Miel, Benalmádena.
Tel. 952 597 016
http://tivolicostadelsol.com
Sevilla
Parque Temático Isla Mágica
Wide variety of attractions, based on the history of Seville and the New World. Open from April to early November.
Isla de la Cartuja s/n.
Tel. 902 161 716
http://islamagica.es

Golf course, Marbella ▼

Practical information

How to get there

By Air
www.aena.es
Almería Airport
Carretera de Níjar km 9. Tel. 950 213 700
Cordoba Airport
Llanos del Castillo. Tel. 957 214 100
Granada Airport
Autovía A-92, next to Chauchina.
Tel. 958 245 200
Jerez de la Frontera Airport
Carretera N-IV. Tel. 956 150 083
Malaga Airport
Aeropuerto Pablo Ruiz Picasso. Avenida
García Morato s/n. Tel. 952 048 484
Seville Airport
Aeropuerto de San Pablo. Carretera N-IV
km 532. Tel. 954 449 000

Train
Renfe (Red Nacional de Ferrocarriles)
AVE (Tren de Alta Velocidad Española)
Tel. 902 240 202
www.renfe.es / www.eltren.com
Almería
Main Railway Station (Renfe).
Plaza de la Estación
Renfe Office. Calle Alcalde Muñoz, 7.
Tel. 950 231 822
Cadiz
Main Railway Station (Renfe).
Plaza de Sevilla. Tel. 956 254 301
Córdoba
Main Railway Station (Renfe and the AVE).
Plaza de las Tres Culturas. Tel. 957 400 202
Granada
Main Railway Station (Renfe). Avenida de los
Andaluces. Tel. 958 271 272
Huelva
Main Railway Station (Renfe). Avenida de
Italia. Tel. 959 245 614
Jaén
Estación Jaén-Espeluy. Renfe, Paseo de la
Estación. Tel 953 270 202
Malaga
Main Railway Station (Renfe and local trains).
Explanada de la Estación. Tel. 952 360 202

Seville
Santa Justa Station. Avenida de Kansas City.
Tel. 954 414 111

Buses
Almería
Bus Station. Tel. 950 262 098
Cadiz
Bus Station. Tel. 956 211 763
Córdoba
Bus Station. Tel. 957 404 040
Granada
Bus Station. Tel. 958 185 480
Huelva
Bus Station. Tel. 959 256 900
Jaén
Bus Station. Tel. 953 250 106
Málaga
Bus Station. Tel. 952 872 657
Seville
Plaza de Armas Station.
Tel. 954 908 040
Prado de San Sebastián Station.
Tel. 954 417 111

Taxi Telephone Numbers
Almería. Tel. 950 251 122/950 301 221
Cadiz. Tel. 956 212 121
Córdoba. Tel. 957 764 444
Granada. Tel. 958 280 654
Huelva. Tel. 959 251 500/959 250 022
Jaén. Tel. 953 222 222
Malaga. Tel. 952 333 333/952 040 804
Seville. Tel. 954 580 000/954 675 555
/954 622 222

Useful Telefone Numbers
Information: 11824/11888
Traffic: Tel. 900 123 505
Medical Emergencies: Tel. 061
Police: Tel. 091 y 092
Guardia Civil: Tel. 062
Firemen: Tel. 080

Tourist Offices
Almería
Parque Nicolás Salmerón. Tel. 950 274 355
Avenida F. García Lorca, Edificio Mirador de
la Rambla. Tel. 950 280 748
Cadiz
Avenida Ramón de Carranza s/n.
Tel. 956 258 646
Plaza San Juan de Dios, 11.
Tel. 956 241 001
Córdoba
Calle Torrijos, 10. Tel 957 471 235
Caballerizas Reales s/n. Tel. 957 200 522
Granada
Corral del Carbón. Mariana Pineda s/n.
Tel 958 221 022
Plaza Mariana Pineda, 10.
Tel. 958 247 128
Huelva
Avenida de Alemania, 14.
Tel. 959 257 403
Jaén
Calle Arquitecto Berges, 1. Tel. 953 222 737
Calle Maestra, 18. Tel. 953 219 116
Malaga
Avenida Cervantes, 1. Tel. 952 604 410
Pasaje de Chinitas, 4. Tel. 952 213 445

Field of sunflowers ▼

Hotel Alfonso XIII, Seville ▲

Seville
Avenida de la Constitución, 21.
Tel. 954 22 14 04
Calle Arjona, 28. Tel. 954 221 714
Plaza del Triunfo, 1. Tel. 954 210 005

Andalucía Online
www.andalucia.org
www.almeria-turismo.org
www.cadizturismo.com
www.turiscordoba.es
www.granada.org
www.ayuntamientohuelva.es
www.promojaen.es
www.malagaturismo.com/
www.webmalaga.com
www.sevilla.org/www.turismosevilla.org

Where to stay

Almería
Gran Hotel Almería (****)
Avenida Reina Regente, 8. Tel. 950 238 011
Hotel Torreluz IV (****)
Plaza de las Flores, 5. Tel. 950 234 999
Hotel Vincci Mediterráneo (****)
Avenida del Mediterráneo s/n.
Tel. 950 624 272
Hotel Costasol (***)
Paseo de Almería, 58. Tel. 950 234 011
Hotel Torreluz III (***)
Plaza de las Flores, 3. Tel. 950 234 399

Cádiz
Parador Hotel Atlántico (****)

Avenida Duque de Nájera, 9.
Tel. 956 226 908
Hotel Tryp la Caleta (****)
Avenida Amílcar Barca s/n. Tel. 956 279 411
Hotel Francia y París (***)
Plaza de San Francisco, 2. Tel. 956 222 348
Hotel Regio (**)
Calle Ana de Viya, 11. Tel. 956 279 331

Córdoba
Parador la Arruzafa (****)
Avenida de la Arruzafa s/n. Tel. 957 275 900
Hotel Abetos del Maestre Escuela (****)
Avenida San José de Calasanz s/n.
Tel. 957 282 105
Hotel Maciá Alfaros (****)
Calle Alfaros, 18. Tel. 957 491 920
NH Amistad Córdoba (****)
Plaza de Maimónides, 3. Tel. 957 420 335
Hotel Maimónides (***)
Calle Torrijos, 4. Tel. 957 471 500
Hotel Albucasis (**)
Calle Buen Pastor, 11. Tel. 957 478 625

Granada
Parador de San Francisco (****)
Real de la Alhambra s/n. Tel. 958 221 440
Hotel Alhambra Palace (****)
Calle Peña Partida, 2-4. Tel. 958 221 468
Hotel Meliá Granada (****)
Calle Ángel Ganivet, 7. Tel. 958 227 400
Hotel Casa del Capitel Nazarí (***)
Cuesta Aceituneros, 6. Tel. 958 215 260
Hotel Palacio de Santa Inés (***)
Cuesta de Santa Inés, 9. Tel. 958 22 23 62

Hotel Reina Cristina (***)
Calle Tablas, 4. Tel. 958 253 211
Hotel Washington Irving (***)
Paseo del Generalife, 2. Tel. 958 227 550
Los Chapiteles (***)
Camino de la Fuente del Avellano s/n.
Tel. 958 220 177
Hotel América (*)
Real de la Alhambra, 53.
Tel. 958 227 471

Huelva
Hotel NH Luz Huelva (****)
Alameda Sundheim, 26. Tel. 959 250 011
Hotel Monte Conquero (***)
Calle Pablo Rada, 10. Tel. 959 285 500
Hotel Tartessos (***)
Avenida Martín Alonso Pinzón, 13.
Tel. 959 282 711
Hotel Costa de la Luz (**)
Calle Alcalde José María del Amo, 8.
Tel. 959 253 214
Hotel Los Condes (**)
Alameda Sundheim, 14. Tel. 959 282 400

Jaén
Parador Santa Catalina (****)
Castillo de Santa Catalina. Tel. 953 230 000
Hotel Infanta Cristina (****)
Avenida de Madrid s/n. Tel. 953 263 040
Hotel Condestable Iranzo (***)
Paseo de la Estación, 32. Tel. 953 222 800
Hotel Husa Europa (***)
Plaza de Belén, 1. Tel. 953 222 700
Hotel Xauen (***)
Plaza del Deán Mazas, 3. Tel 953 240 789

Malaga
Parador de Gibralfaro (****)
Castillo de Gibralfaro s/n. Tel. 952 221 902
Hotel AC Málaga Palacio (****)
Calle Cortina del Muelle, 1. Tel. 952 215 185
Hotel Larios (****)
Calle Marqués de Larios, 2. Tel. 952 222 200
Hotel NH Málaga (****)
Avenida del Río Guadalmedina s/n.
Tel. 952 071 323
Hotel Tryp Alameda (****)
Avenida de la Aurora, 25. Tel. 952 368 020
Hotel Don Curro (***)
Calle Sancha de Lara, 7. Tel. 952 227 200
Hotel Las Vegas (***)
Paseo de Sancha, 22. Tel. 952 217 712
Hotel Los Naranjos (***)
Paseo de Sancha, 35. Tel. 952 224 316

Craft shop, Frigiliana, Málaga ▲

Hotel California (**)
Paseo de Sancha, 17. Tel. 952 215 165

Seville
Hotel Alfonso XIII (*****GL)
Calle San Fernando, 2. Tel. 954 917 000
Hotel Casa Imperial (*****)
Calle Imperial, 29. Tel. 954 500 300
Hotel AC Ciudad de Sevilla (****)
Avenida Manuel Siurot, 25. Tel. 954 230 505
Hotel Bécquer (****)
Calle Reyes Católicos, 4. Tel. 954 228 900
Hotel Hesperia Sevilla (****)
Avenida Eduardo Dato, 49. Tel. 954 548 300
Hotel Las Casas del Rey de Baeza (****)
Plaza Jesús de la Redención, 2.
Tel. 954 561 496
Hotel Meliá Sevilla (****)
Calle Pedro de Castro, 1. Tel. 954 421 511
Hotel Rey Alfonso X (****)
Calle Ximénez de Enciso, 35.
Tel. 954 21 00 70
Hotel San Gil (****)
Calle Parras, 28. Tel. 954 906 811
Hotel Las Casas de la Judería (***)
Santa María la Blanca-Callejón de Dos
Hermanas, 7. Tel. 954 415 150
Hotel Las Casas de los Mercaderes (***)
Calle Álvarez Quintero, 9. Tel. 954 225 858
Hotel NH Plaza de Armas (***)
Calle Marqués de Paradas s/n.
Tel. 954 901 992
Hotel Amadeus (**)
Calle Farnesio, 6. Tel. 954 501 443

Hotel Simón (*)
Calle García de Vinuesa, 19.
Tel. 954 226 660

● **Restaurants and Bars**

Almería
Building
Paseo Marítimo s/n. Tel. 950 261 204
El Bello Rincón
Carretera N-340 km 436. Tel. 950 238 427
Rincón de Juan Pedro
Plaza del Carmen. Tel. 950 235 819
Terraza Carmona
Calle Manuel Giménez, 1. Tel. 950 390 760
Valentín
Calle Tenor Iribarne, 19. Tel. 950 264 475

Cadiz
Achuri
Calle Plocia, 15. Tel. 956 253 613
El Faro
Calle San Félix, 15. Tel. 956 211 068
El Ventorrillo del Chato
Carretera Cádiz-San Fernando, km 2.
Tel. 956 250 025
La Comercial
Calle José del Toro, 8. Tel. 956 211 914
San Antonio
Plaza de San Antonio, 9. Tel. 956 212 680

Córdoba
Almudaina
Campo Santo de los Mártires, 1.
Tel. 957 474 342
Bodegas Campos
Calle Lineros, 32. Tel. 957 497 500
Casa Pepe de la Judería
Calle Romero, 1. Tel. 957 200 744
El Caballo Rojo
Calle Cardenal Herrero, 28. Tel. 957 475 375
El Churrasco
Calle Romero, 16. Tel. 957 290 819

Granada
Alhacena de las Monjas
Plaza Padre Suárez, 5. Tel. 958 221 105
Carmen de San Miguel
Plaza de Torres Bermejas, 3. Tel. 958 226 723
Cunini
Plaza de la Pescadería, 9. Tel. 958 250 777
Chikito
Plaza del Campillo, 9. Tel 958 223 364
Mirador de Morayma
Pianista García Carrillo, 2. Tel. 958 228 290

Las Tinajas
Calle Martínez Campos, 17. Tel. 958 254 393
Los Manueles
Calle Zaragoza, 2-4. Tel 958 223 415
Sevilla
Calle Oficios, 12. Tel. 958 221 223

Huelva
El Estero
Avenida Martín Alonso Pinzón, 13.
Tel. 959 256 572
El Portichuelo
Avenida Martín Alonso Pinzón, 1.
Tel. 959 245 768
Las Candelas
Carretera Aljaraque-Punta Umbría.
Tel. 959 318 301
La Esquinita
Calle Béjar, 21. Tel. 959 252 690
Las Meigas
Avenida de Guatemala, 48. Tel. 959 271 958

Jaén
Az-Zait
Calle Ceuta s/n. Tel. 953 263 040
Casa Antonio
Calle Fermín Palma, 3. Tel. 953 270 262
Casa Vicente
Calle Francisco Martín Mora, 1.
Tel. 953 232 222
Mesón Nuyra
Pasaje Nuyra s/n. Tel. 953 240 763
Parador Santa Catalina
Castillo de Santa Catalina.
Tel. 953 230 000

Sardines on skewers ▼

Restaurant, Hotel Alfonso XIII, Seville ▲

and Ronda de los Tejares. The area around the Mosque has numerous small craft shops, as does the Municipal Market in the calle Judiós. On Tuesdays and Fridays there is a second-hand market in the Jardín quarter.

Granada
The main shopping area in Granada is located in the centre from the Gran Vía to Puerta Real and the surrounding streets. There are numerous craft and souvenir shops in the Albayzín and the streets leading up to the Alhambra, also to be found in the Alcaicería, the Zacatín and the area around the Cathedral. In the Chana quarter a second-hand market is held on Wednesdays, and another in the Zaidín on Saturdays.

Huelva
Most shops are located around the centre of town on the calle Concepción, the Plaza de las Monjas and the Gra Vía and nearby streets. Nearby is the Mercado del Carmen with its excellent fish and seafood.

Jaén
The old city centre around the Plaza de Santa María has the traditional shops, while more modern ones are to be found on the calle Nueva, the Avenida de la Estación and Avenida de Madrid. There is a second-hand market on Thursdays in the fair complex.

Malaga
Malaga has a large area of varied shops and shopping centres extending from the calle Marqués de Larios and nearby streets in the city centre to the Alamada Principal and the Guadalmedina.

Seville
The southern part of the old city centre houses most of the traditional shops, extending from the Avenida de la Constitución, the Plaza Nueva, the calles Sierpes and Tetuán to the Plaza del Duque. There are numerous craft shops in the Santa Cruz quarter while the Nervión area has another modern shopping precinct. On Thursdays the calle Feria has a second-hand and antiques markets, while on Sundays there is an animal market in the Plaza de la Alfalfa and a collectors' market in the Plaza del Cabildo.

Malaga
Adolfo
Paseo Marítimo P. Ruiz Picasso, 12.
Tel. 952 601 914
Antonio Martín
Plaza de la Malagueta s/n. Tel. 952 227 398
Café de París
Calle Vélez Málaga, 8. Tel. 952 225 043
Casa Pedro
Calle Quitapenas, 121. Tel. 952 290 013
El Chinitas
Calle Moreno Monroy, 4. Tel. 952 210 972
La Casa del Ángel
Calle Madre de Dios, 29. Tel. 952 608 750
La Cónsula
Finca la Cónsula, Churriana. Tel. 952 622 562
Parador de Gibralfaro
Castillo de Gibralfaro. Tel. 952 221 902
Refectorium
Calle Cervantes, 8. Tel. 952 218 990

Seville
Casablanca
Calle Zaragoza, 50. Tel. 954 224 698
Casa Robles
Calle Álvarez Quintero, 58. Tel. 954 563 272
Egaña Oriza
Calle San Fernando, 41. Tel. 954 227 211
Enrique Becerra
Calle Gamazo, 2. Tel. 954 213 049
La Albahaca
Plaza de Santa Cruz, 9. Tel. 954 220 714
La Alquería
Hacienda Benazuza, Sanlúcar la Mayor.
Tel. 955 703 344
La Isla
Calle Arfe, 25. Tel. 954 212 621

La Judería
Calle Cano y Cueto, 13. Tel. 954 412 052
Poncio
Calle Victoria, 8. Tel. 954 340 010
Sabina
Calle Dos de Mayo, 4. Tel. 945 562 547
San Fernando 27
Calle San Fernando, 27. Tel. 954 220 966
San Marco
Calle Cuna, 6. Tel. 954 212 4 40
Taberna del Alabardero
Calle Zaragoza, 20. Tel. 954 37

● Shopping

Almería
The Calle de las Tiendas, the Puerta de Purchena and the Paseo de Almería are the best known and most central shopping areas in Almería, while around the Rambla de Belén the most up-to-date shops are to be found. The Mercado de Abastos (Food Market) is certainly worth a look.

Cádiz
The traditional shops in Cadiz are to be found in the old part of town, around the calles Ancha, Rosario and Sacramento, while the more modern shops are along the Avenida de Andalucía and nearby streets. The food market is near the Plaza de las Flores. The Avenida de Guadalquivir is the location for the famous Piojito second-hand market.

Córdoba
The modern shopping area is around the calles Cruz Conde, Concepción, Gondomar

Edited and produced by: **Ediciones Aldeasa**
Translation: **Laura Suffield**
Design: **Antonio Ochoa de Zabalegui**
Layout: **José María Carrizo**
Film-making: **Lucam**
Printing: **TF. Artes Gráficas**

© of this edition, Aldeasa 2004
© of the texts and translations, the authors
© of the authorised reproductions:
Aldeasa: 28, 29, 30, 31, 32, 33, 34, 35, 36, 38, 39, 40, 66, 74b, 74c, 75,
76, 88b, 89, 122, 123, 124, 127, 128 a, 129, 130, 131, 135 a, 150, 151b, 155.
Hidalgo-Lopesino: 4, 6, 8, 45, 46, 48, 49, 50, 52, 53, 54, 57, 58, 60, 61,
62, 63, 64, 65, 68, 69, 70, 71, 72, 73, 74 a, 80, 81, 82 b, 83 b, 84, 85,
86 b, 87, 88 a, 92, 98 b, 99 a, 109, 111, 114, 115, 116, 126, 132, 133, 134,
135 b, 136, 137, 138, 139, 142, 143, 144, 145, 146, 147, 148, 149, 151 a,
152, 153, 154, 156.
César Justel: 44, 100, 102 a, 103, 141.
Covadonga de Noriega: 10, 12, 13, 14, 15, 16, 17, 18, 19, 20, 21, 22, 23, 24, 25,
41, 42, 43, 55, 56, 78, 82 a, 83 a, 86 a, 93, 94, 95, 96, 97, 98 a, 99 b, 101, 102 b,
104, 106, 108, 110, 112, 113, 117, 118, 119, 128 b.

I.S.B.N: 84-8003-449-1
Depósito legal: M-16744-2004